Just Like That!

On the night of 15 April 1984, on the stage of Her Majesty's Theatre in London, Tommy Cooper suffered a heart attack in front of millions of television viewers. He died shortly afterwards.

TOMMY COOPER HAS ALSO WRITTEN:

Three letters to his wife,
Several hundred ditto *to the tax man,*
A postcard to his dog,
Football coupons and pre-paid business replies,
And on the back of his hand:
                    REMEMBER THE LAUNDRY OR ELSE!

Just Like That!

An Autobiography . . .
of Sorts

Tommy Cooper

This edition published in Great Britain in 1994 by
Virgin Books
an imprint of Virgin Publishing Ltd
332 Ladbroke Grove
London W10 5AH

Published in 1976 by Wyndham Publications Ltd
Reprinted in 1984 by the Paperback Division of W H Allen & Co

First published as *Tommy Cooper Jokes and Tricks: Just Like That!* in 1975
by Jupiter Books (London) Limited

Text copyright © Virgin Publishing Ltd 1994
Cover photograph copyright © Scope Features
Text photographs copyright © Thames Television

A catalogue record for this book is available from the British Library

ISBN 0 86369 852 2

Typeset by Litho Link Ltd, Welshpool, Powys
Printed and bound in Great Britain by Cox & Wyman Ltd, Reading, Berks

This book is dedicated

Contents

A SPECIAL ANNOUNCEMENT . . .

BEFORE I START I WOULD LIKE TO PUT THE RECORD
STRAIGHT. ON MONDAY, 10 FEBRUARY 1975, BILL HAGERTY IN
THE *Daily Mirror* REPORTED THAT I HAD BEEN WINDOW
SHOPPING AND BOUGHT FOUR WINDOWS. THIS WAS NOT
QUITE TRUE. I DID BUY FOUR, BUT RETURNED ONE. IT WAS
CRACKED.

Introduction

ONE DAY I WAS hanging about thinking of this and that and not much else, when I suddenly thought to myself, why not write a book. Why not, indeed? Straight away I sat down with pen and paper and wrote nearly one hundred pages on why not.

The fact is, I've always wanted to write something. Everyone does. You've only got to go into a public place and you can see what struggling would-be writers are trying to get out. For example, on one wall I saw written, 'Smoking stunts your growth'. Below it, about two feet off the ground, someone else had written, 'Now he tells me.'

The fact is, there are poems and all sorts of interesting items, complete with illustrations, to be found on walls. This goes to show how many budding authors there are and I know they really appreciate their readers. I once saw a beautifully written notice on the wall of a little place beneath Tottenham Court Road which simply said, 'We wish all our readers a Merry Christmas.' I thought it charming. It expressed the depth of feeling that exists between writer and reader.

Anyway, I gave a good deal of thought to this writing business. I thought, what can I write about? I mean, I've been around. I've tried my hand at all sorts of jobs. You wouldn't believe it. For instance, I once had a job painting the white lines down roadways. I packed it in before I went round the bend. Then there was a job where

3

I took things easy and the next job where they locked everything away.

Should I write about the funny people I've met in my time? Like the cat burglar. He stole hundreds of cats. He was politically motivated. He was a Meeowist. And what about the Siamese Twins who held up a bank? They didn't wear stocking masks. They shared a pair of tights. I knew a cannibal who was fond of titbits and his brother who had been influenced by Catholic missionaries: on Fridays he only ate fishermen. I once fought a boxer with an ingrowing nose and ingrowing ears. I lived next door to a van driver who was always smashing into the backs of vans. He was a vandal. Nobody wanted any truck with him.

Now, I've been interested in jokes and tricks all my life. I was always reading books about jokes and tricks. At school, my teacher said I was a very tricky customer and that she thought my schoolwork was just a big joke. I once knew a man who did tricks with saucers. He was a sorcerer. Another chap I knew did tricks with jugs. He was a juggler. Then it came to me in a flash. It was a flash in the pen. I would write about jokes and tricks. After all, that is what life is all about when you think about it. So that's what I've done.

I would like finally to recall those immortal words said to me by a bookie – words I've never forgotten – 'All the world's a stooge, and all the men and women in it, merely horseplayers.' Well, I'm fond of a bit of the old horseplay myself, so here's the book I've written. If you don't like it, there's nothing I can do about it now,* except to wish you all a merry Christmas!

* But perhaps the publisher can! Contact *him*.

4

1

Cooper

M Y FATHER SAID the day I was born was a red letter
day. He received final demands for the gas,
electricity, rates and half a dozen assorted H.P. items. As
I popped into the world, blinking at the light and
wondering what to do for an encore, someone grabbed
me by the legs, held me upside down and whacked me
jolly hard. That was just for starters. Already I could see
life was not going to be easy. I cried like a baby. Is it any
wonder I soon took to the bottle?

I was nearly a step-child. I heard some old biddy say to
my mother:

'You've got a right one here.'

'He'll be a left one,' said my mother. 'Left on
someone's doorstep if I get half a chance. He's a mark of
my shame. He's a crying shame. Shove him back in the
rack, mark him "reject", or file him or something.'

Well, infants have their infantry, and adults have their
adultery. Such is life.

I tried my first trick when I was six months old. I
pulled the tablecloth from the table. I meant the tea things
to remain where they were. It did not work too well and
some of my mother's best china was bent. I didn't get a
laugh, even though I wore my potty for a hat and did an
impersonation of John Hanson singing 'The Ballad of
Eskimo Nell'.

My next trick was when I put the cat among the
pigeons. It was enough to make any cat laugh. Ours was

5

a Cheshire cat anyway. Nobody else laughed, although the trick worked. I had made the pigeons disappear. I thought I could get a big laugh throwing custard pies. But there weren't any handy, so I threw my mum's rock cakes. She used to make them with real rocks. She also made sponge cakes with real sponges. Dad was displeased. One rock cake hit him on the ear and broke his deaf aid. He couldn't hear the racing results on the radio. I was a year old.

When I was three, my parents, with much difficulty, managed to get me into a kindergarten or play centre, as it is now called. I had less trouble in getting out . . .

I was a big lad by the time I started primary school. I sang in the school choir until I was six. Then my voice broke. I was becoming more and more interested in magic. We had a boy in our class who could throw his voice. He used to drink a gottle of geer every day. He got us into trouble for talking in class without any of us saying a word. I put a stop to his capers with my big magic trick. I sawed him in half.

The boys called me bighead behind my back. Never to my face. They would just walk up to me and whisper 'Psst! Keep this under your hat,' and hand me a football. I played football for the school team once only. I scored four goals. Our team lost, four goals to nil. I never wanted to be a footballer, anyway. I didn't like all that kissing and cuddling. My friend, Mike Meller, was good at football and not much else. His father was a doctor.

He went home one day and said,

'Is it right Dad, one and one make two?'

'Yes,' said his father.

'And two and two make four?', said Mike.

'Right,' said the doctor.

'That's exactly what the teacher said,' said Mike. 'I just wanted a second opinion.'

Mind you, Mike knew all about sex, but I found sex education very confusing. I remember going home from school and asking my mother who was the opposite sex, she or dad?

I had another friend at school, we called him Tadpole. When he grew up he became a frogman. I used to play conkers with him. I always won. I used a coconut. I got half a dozen of them in a pennyworth of mixed nuts.

At school I was interested in handicrafts, woodcraft, metalcraft, paper craft – all sorts of crafts. My teacher said I was the craftiest boy in the school. I once went on a student cruise on a liner. It was a scholarship. I also sailed through my exams.

Ours was a normal household. Much the same as anyone else's. My mother cooked the meals, my father pottered about the house. His pots were everywhere. One day I came home from school for dinner.

'What's this?' I asked my mother, 'I thought we were having liver today.'

'So you are, in a way,' said my mum. 'The cat ate the liver. We're eating the cat.' She was always pulling my leg. That's why one is six inches longer than the other.

My father decided to do up the inside of the house. He sent me to the 'Do It Yourself Shop' for some fatters. His paint was too thin. A man came to help him. I knew he was a painter. He had two coats. Dad was using a drill and it caught fire. It was a fire drill. While he was knocking holes in the wall my mother handed him a bill. It gave him a shock. It was an electric bill. My father said the next time the man came to read the electric meter he would give him enough flex to electrocute himself.

7

My dad carpeted the house from top to bottom. Then he found he had laid the carpet upside down. We were the only house in the street with wall to wall rubber. You couldn't hear yourself walk. When he plastered the ceiling he used sticking plaster. One day he was painting the front door. There was a sudden disturbance. It was the Mad Parson from Parson's Green. He was singing. I could tell he was a parson, by his nose. He wanted to use our phone to call his brother in Scotland. He said it was a parson to parson call. My father was a hospitable sort of chap. He asked my mother to fix them some drinks. He had a whisky mac. The parson had a Holy Mary. That's vodka without the tomato juice and Worcestershire.

I joined the Scouts. In those days they wore shorts. They were all right for a knees-up but not flattering for my image. Anyway, I started off with a bang. One of the Scout tests was to make a fire by rubbing two sticks together. I used two sticks of dynamite. I was told to pitch a tent. There was no pitch so I used creosote. I had a brand new Scout knife. It had a gadget for removing stones from horses' hooves. I spent a fortnight looking for a horse and when I found one it didn't have a single stone in its hooves. It wasn't time wasted. Our rhubarb did well out of it.

But I did make a mess of the knot tying. It was a real bind and I finished up by telling the Scoutmaster to get knotted. I was drummed out of the troop.

After that I took up boxing. My trainer said I was a real slugger. I was very unlucky with my opponents. The first was a panel-beater, and he beat the hell out of me. The next was a punch operator. He punched holes in me. Another chap I fought was a milkman. I was told he couldn't punch his way out of a paper bag. He punched the whey out of me.

My second said to me, 'All you have to do is go out there and if he hits you, hit him right back.' I went out to the centre of the ring and danced around. I got giddy and fell through the ropes. My second forced me back into the ring. The milkman said 'Milko!' and knocked me bowlegged. I made a grab at him. He yelled. I had him by the shorts. We fell to the canvas. He got up first, but I still had his shorts. He was carried from the ring wrapped in a blanket. He was declared the winner, on points. I came second. The last person I fought was a curate. He was a Bible puncher.

When we lived in Southampton I used to see a lot of sailors. I once saw Barnacle Bill the sailor, Popeye the sailor, and Sinbad the sailor. They drank a mixture of rum and seawater, sea-shandies. I once saw Barnacle Bill blowing a trumpet. Smoke was coming out of it. It was a horn-pipe.

We had a dog. My father took it out for a walk one night. He was stopped by a policeman.

'Hey,' yelled the policeman. 'Watch it! if I catch you again allowing that dog to foul the pavement, I'll run you straight in. Your feet won't touch the ground. You train your dog to do it in the gutter.'

A few weeks later dad met the same policeman.

'Hello! Hello Hello!' said the copper, bouncing up and down on the balls of his feet, 'Where's your dog?'

'Dead!' said dad.

'Ha-ha!' said the copper. 'Sorry to hear that. How did that happen then?'

'Well,' said dad, 'I was training him to go in the gutter, like you said, and he fell off the roof. Ha-ha yourself, mister special clever cop.'

My dad appeared at the magistrate's court. He wasn't there two minutes. It was a brief case.

We got a police dog after that. His name was Rex. He used to stand by our front gate and arrest other dogs for loitering with intent. One of our neighbours complained that our dog had bitten his elbow. Dad said he couldn't understand it as he had trained the dog to start at the bottom. Dad took Rex to the vet. He said that the trouble with Rex was that he could tell an arm from an elbow. The vet was reputed to be wonderful to his wife. He treated her just like a dog.

2

Cooper the Trooper

THE DAY I JOINED the army I was interviewed by a Colour-Sergeant in the Guards. He asked me if I could ride or did I know anything about horses. I said I didn't. He said, 'You seem to me to be a little hoarse,' and put me in the Horse Guards. I then had a test to see if I could swear like a trooper.

I was sent to the cavalry barracks at Aldershot. There was a shortage of space. Most of us shared the stables with the horses. The horses complained. Several soldiers had to be billeted in the fields. They were un-stable. The unit I reported to had only one horse in the beginning. It was a one horse outfit.

Eventually we did get some more horses, but all I got was Raymond, the troop mascot, he was a little donkey. My feet touched the ground on either side of him. Whenever the bugle sounded the charge, off would go the troop in every direction, and Raymond would go trotting off leaving me standing bow-legged. The Corporal would then shout 'Whoa! Hold your horses', and I would cradle little Raymond in my arms. Eventually I got a horse, and Raymond was transferred. One day the Sergeant-Major yelled to me 'Cooper! What is your donkey doing in the company office?'

'He's been promoted,' I said. 'He was officer material. He's there to do the donkey work.'

'All right', said the Sergeant-Major, 'but he'll have to watch out for the Adjutant. He might talk the hind leg off

11

him. We haven't much use for a three legged donkey, except, maybe, in the inter-regimental three-legged race, which isn't a bad idea at that.'

Most of the troopers were getting bow-legged. If we were going to a dance we used to straighten our legs by clutching a saveloy between our knees and stretching it down between our ankles. Then we would jump up and down to a couple of choruses of 'Knees-up Mother Brown'.

We had a trooper named Skimpole. He was the fastest thing on two legs. We all felt sorry for his horse. Have you ever seen a horse with a hernia? Another trooper had been transferred from the RAF. He always sat on his horse backwards. He had been a tail-gunner. He used to keep falling from his horse, so they fastened him to the saddle with a strap. Another trooper was a Pole. He was a gallup Pole.

I soon found that old troopers never tossed a coin to decide anything. They just shouted, 'Heads or tails?' and tossed a horse. One time I was riding an old grey mare, but it turned out she wasn't what she used to be. I was switched to a great big black stallion. This was a horse of a different colour. It was a real dark horse. After him I had a gelding. It was specially cut out for the job.

The Corporal of the Horse Guards was always picking on me. One day as I was walking across the barrack square he yelled 'Hey, Cooper! I know the regimental mascot died, but that was last year. You don't still have to walk around with your trousers at half mast. And empty your pockets. They look like saddle bags.' My pockets were empty at the time.

The Corporal said he had been born in the saddle. It must have been hard on his mother. He once asked me to go to the store to get him a pair of riding boots.

'Yes, Corp.', I said, 'West Riding or South Riding?'

When I came back he complained that the boots squeaked.

'You wouldn't just squeak,' I said, 'you would yell if some clodhopper walked on you.'

We found barrack life very humdrum. Whenever we went on parade there would be a lot of humming and hawing. We would hum and the horses would haw. Sometimes we would just horse about.

Finally I got a horse with a very soft saddle. It was a saddle of mutton. One day I was mounting up. I had one foot in the stirrup when the horse galloped off like balmy. I hopped alongside him for a mile or two but in the end it became quite a drag. I woke up in military hospital. It was so quiet you could hear a pin drop. Then I heard a man singing a sea shanty. He had been in the navy, in the submarine cavalry. They rode sea horses. He was suffering from land sickness.

Our officers were a strange lot. One, we used to call Beryl, was drummed out of the service. He was caught riding side-saddle. We used to call the officers the 'Scilly Brigade'. We had a captain with a fantastic walrus moustache. How he got it was a closely guarded military secret. Most of the men thought he had pinched it from a real walrus and had it grafted around his nose. But I discovered his secret. He had gone to the doctor with an ingrowing hair up his nostril only to discover it was a complete ingrowing moustache. The doctor had operated on him to turn his face inside out. He had been a schoolmaster and always carried a cane. He would whack anyone within striking distance and shout, 'That hurt me

13

more than it hurt you', and then burst into tears. We believed him. In fact we always felt sorry for him.

We had an officer from the Shetlands who always rode a Shetland pony. He was unpopular because of the deep depression that was always hanging over him. He always wore a superior smile when he went riding. Most everyone else wore riding breeches.

I had a lazy horse. Everything was too much trouble for him. Instead of carrying me, most of the time I had to carry *him*. I was the only trooper with saddle sores on his shoulders. He was a queer animal. He wasn't fond of oats, but he could stand a lot of chaff.

We were finally mechanized. We were issued with tanks. The men soon got used to them, but the horses found them a bit cramped. So we gave the soldier's farewell to our steeds; our steeds gave us the horse laugh and we soon found ourselves in the Middle East with a war on.

We went into camp near the Suez. It was no holiday camp, not like the posters at all. I went on parade wearing shorts for the first time since my Boy Scout days. My under-pants kept sticking out.

'Cooper!' yelled the corporal, 'your bloomers are sticking out!'

'Never mind the bloomers.' I yelled back, 'my stays are killing me.'

I got seven days jankers.

While in this camp we played cricket against a battalion from Palestine. When our captain yelled for a new ball, they offered to accept the old one in part-exchange.

We had a General visit us at our camp. He came to the men's mess and took a big dollop from a tin.

'Ah! This is very good butter,' he said. 'Very good butter, to be sure.'

One of the officers hurriedly pointed out that it was axle-grease.

'Ah,' exclaimed the General, 'this is very good axle-grease,' and he helped himself to another mouthful.

He spotted me as I was leaving the mess tent.

'Who is that man with the two concertinas hanging from his belt?' he demanded. My trousers did need pressing. He had our Intelligence Officer with him. He was disguised as a worm, to worm his way into our confidence. He got me another seven days jankers.

Once we were lost in the middle of the desert. There we were not knowing in which direction to go. We tried to work it out by a process of elimination. We knew we didn't want to go up. We knew we didn't want to go down. That got rid of two possibilities for a start.

Suddenly we saw a penguin waddling towards us. We thought it must be a mirage. But it turned out to be a waiter from the Normandy Hotel in Cairo. He had stepped out of the kitchen, across the garden and got lost. The steak and chips were cold but they went down all right. We finally reached this little oasis. There were no girls but there were plenty of dates.

The next morning, on the horizon, there was a row of camels. What a sight! It was a caravan site. One of the caravans had an ad in the window, 'Room for rent. Must be willing to travel.'

A little man came up to me and whispered in my ear.

'Psst, effendi! Do you want to buy a piano? It fell off the back of a camel.'

I played in a few shows for troops in Cairo. One of the most popular ditties at the time was a little number called 'Up your pipe, King Farouk,' dedicated to the then King of Egypt, and which the British Tommies always sang with gusto on every special occasion as a mark of respect. One of my friends, he had a smoke-curing factory in Blighty, opened up a smoke house in Cairo for smoking camel. He reckoned it would be the biggest thing since smoked salmon. He said that smoked camel sandwiches were a natural. He got the idea from an American poster he saw in Cairo which said 'Smoke Camels'.

About that time I started wearing my fez at army shows. I used to grow geraniums in it. I also got up to my old tricks. I didn't pull rabbits out of a hat. They never know when to stop. I pulled a pig out of a poke. Once I pulled a reindeer out of a hat. It was a deerstalker. I tried sawing a lady in half but didn't know what to do with the bits. I wound up the act by letting the cat out of the bag. It was a howling success.

3

Cooper the Trouper

AFTER I LEFT the army I decided to go on the boards. I went to see an agent and showed him my routine.

'Well?' I asked. 'What do you think of that then?'

Funny man! I couldn't understand a word he said. He had a peg on his nose.

While I was there, another man came in for an audition. He actually flew round the room three times whistling 'Only a Bird in a Gilded Cage', and landed on the ceiling. Marvellous! The agent turned him down. He said that bird acts were two a penny. I also saw him turn down a talking dog who danced the tango, because he didn't like his legs. I later found this agent was a secret agent from MI5. He knew nothing about acts: not even third acts.

But I was soon on the merry-go-round: cabaret, music halls, clubs, TV – the lot. I travelled up and down the country staying at hotels and boarding houses, meeting all kinds of people.

I remember a boarding house in Blackpool where I stayed. The landlord was dogmatic and his wife was bitchy. They hounded me. Every night they used to take each other out, walkies. I must remember to send them a couple of tins of mince chunkies for Christmas.

Sunday dinner there! What a performance! The host would rap out a rapid grace, and then it was every man for himself. Meat, greens and spuds would go flying in all directions. Bits of plastic Yorkshire pudding stuck to the ceiling and gravy slopped all over the table. You had to be quick to dodge the stabbing forks. There's the back of my hand to prove it. For afters there was always something with curdled custard. We never did find out what that something was. We suspected but we didn't care to talk about it.

At one place I stayed in Manchester, we used to have a trapeze artiste who took her meals swinging from the chandelier. There was a contortionist who could look up his own back to see if his hat was on straight. Then there was an hygenic acrobat who used to do handstands on the toilet seat, and a midget who had served in the navy on midget submarines. He was working as a radio repair man inside transistors.

In a Wigan boarding house, we had a man who called himself a lion-tamer. He trained sea-lions. He used to get roaring drunk on sea-shanties. Then there was the xylophone player. He got drunk one night. He tore up a couple of Belisha Beacons and tried to play the overture to *William Tell* on a pedestrian crossing. He had an uncle who was a bird impersonator. He used to go down the Underground and ride round and round the Inner Circle and finally disappear up the Elephant and Castle.

I was once playing in Newcastle when I met a girl who used to be a snake-charmer. She gave it up because the snakes were always messing about. The boarding house where we were staying was strange. All night long I could hear humming but it wasn't until I was bitten I realised it was a humbug. My landlady warned me to watch my step when she found a strange footprint on my hot water-bottle.

While I was at a hotel in Walsall there was a convention going on for fruit growers. The language in the bars was choice and fruity. I was told that the convention turned out to be fruitful. The Shoe Manufacturers' convention, a few weeks before, was a lot of cobblers talking about how they could save their souls. Very religious.

I missed a booking once. I phoned my agent. He said 'What are you getting all steamed up about?' I was phoning from a sauna. He had just booked an ex-policeman who wanted to be an actor. He was tired of being called a pig and preferred to be called a ham for a change. He played straight parts but in the end he turned out to be bent. He stole the show at the Hippodrome, Pudsey.

At Margate I stayed at a hostel. I could tell by the way the tables were laid for dinner that our hostess was well travelled. I had an Iberia knife, an SAS fork and an Air France spoon. It was a jet set. The hostess was blunt about it. She said she didn't like to leave everything in the air. She was an air hostess.

In Wells, the Cathedral town, the landlady at the boarding house where I stayed was a pirate. Her black beard repelled all boarders. The boarders were a motley crowd. There was an impressionist who was always taking off someone or other. One day he took himself off with the wife of his best friend.

There were a couple of acts the talent shows hadn't yet discovered. One even had his own clapometer. An old girl, a Mrs Fargo, known as 'Wells' Fargo, gave drama lessons. She was a stage-coach. She told me about a couple of friars who had gone to work at the local chip shop. One was a fish-friar: the other was a chip-monk.

When I am on tour I like to look around the shops, especially antique shops. I went into one antique shop and bought a music-stand. I couldn't get a note out of it.

The shopkeeper tried to sell me a four-poster bed. I didn't like the posters. He said the bed was ideal for antique lovers. I said I might be old but I wasn't antique yet. I picked up a funny looking article.

'What's this?' I asked.

'Why, it's as plain as a pikestaff,' he said. 'It's a pikestaff!'

I was so annoyed I rammed my pipe into my jacket pocket. My jacket caught fire. It was a blazer.

As I left the shop I bumped into an old acquaintance. He was a soft-shoe dancer. He told me that he had taken a job as a postman. He said it was better than walking the streets. He had just had an operation. An ear transplant. He complained to his surgeon that he could now hear violins playing all the time in that ear. The surgeon said he wasn't surprised. The donor had an ear for music.

I played in a market town in the Black Country. It was a black market. What a reception! The locals showered me with eggs, cream, butter and milk. I was a mess. I went to the gents for a wash and brush up. There were four cubicles. It was a fourflusher. I was flustered. I dropped the brush and I bent to recover it. The seat fell on my head. I staggered out into the corridor to the bar. I bumped into the stage manager.

'Ah, Tommy!' he said. 'You're looking very flushed. Have one on me.'

There was no answer to that.

I made my debut at the London Palladium in 1952. I met an old fellow in the bar who asked me if I were the Tommy Cooper he had just seen on the stage. I said I was and he said it served me right. It turned out that this man had been a missionary many years ago in the Solomon Islands when the islanders were still cannibals. He said it had been the missionaries who had given the cannibals their first taste of religion.

The old missionary told me that life with the cannibals had never been dull. There was always something cooking. The old cannibal chef would often have acquaintances for dinner. The chef's daughter had written a cookbook called *Jungle Cooking or Have Your Friends for Dinner.*

While the old missionary and I were talking, there was a sudden disturbance. It was the Mad Cannibal from Canning Town doing the can-can.

4

Cooper the Duper

I MADE MY FIRST appearance in the USA in 1954. I appeared at the fabulous Hotel Flamingo, Las Vegas. The press said I was the high spot of the show. No wonder, I'm six feet four. The rest of the performers were three feet six. I thought as the hotel was called The Flamingo, I would do my big trick with flamingos instead of doves, but their legs kept sticking out of my coat-tails. So I did the trick with some cards I had met at the swimming pool, they were only three feet six too.

While I was in Las Vegas I was invited to a cocktail party at a nearby motel. It was close to a huge car cemetery. A big notice outside said, RUST IN PIECES.

There I was with a cocktail in one hand and a toothpick in the other, when a woman came hopping up to me. It was Hedda Hopper. She was dodging the column. She was a fifth columnist.

'Ah!' she said, 'you're Mr Cooper I am told. Hi Gary!'

'I'm not that sort of Cooper,' I said.

'Cooper, Cooper!' she said. 'Seen one, seen them all.'

She stuffed an olive in my ear and hopped off.

I met too that great rock-star, Rock Hudson, who had just left his uncle upstairs or downstairs with MacMillan and Wife. Some joker was there too. He was jamming bananas into a fruit machine which was tilted upside down, and he was singing 'I'll do it my way.' He had blue eyes.

An American friend of mine then pointed out a lot of

Mafia men in the lobby of the hotel. There was this man slapping another man around. I asked my friend what it was all about.

'That guy doing the hitting bit,' he said, 'is the ex-boxer, Slapsy the Schlapper. He's a hit man. And that guy there with the size-twelves, that's Harry the Cobbler. He specialises in making concrete boots. The guy he is talking to is Hugh "rat-tat-tat" Ratzoff. He is a Tommy-gunner, so watch out. As a matter of fact, he is the original Hugh dirty rat, Hugh.'

'I like that,' I said, 'but I like the look of that cracker over there better. Who is she?'

'That,' said my friend, 'is Bridget Cardot. She's a hit woman. They call her Contract Bridget.'

'What about that nervous looking fellow over there?' I asked.

'Oh, him!' said my friend. 'You mean the guy flitting around winking and nudging himself? He's nobody. He's in civil engineering. He just supplies cement to Harry the Cobbler.'

'Do you know that girl who just walked in?' I asked.

'Do I?' said my friend. 'Why, that's nobody but Wanda Downtown, the lady cop. Now, she's really something. Have you ever seen a cop with legs like that? She really knows her stuff. When she heard that the local laundromat was being used by crooked politicians to wash their dirty linen, she went to clean up the joint. She took her knuckle-dusters and her bold automatic tucked down her stockings. A reporter spoke to one of the arrested men. He said he didn't want to talk about it, but it was a fair cop.'

'But of course,' continued my friend, 'the case came to nothing. The prosecuting attorney was bought for a song to the tune of "Who wants to be a millionaire? I do." The judge was sewn up tight. In a sack at the bottom of the lake. And do you see the guy with the ears, the nose and that mouth? That's the big shot, No-face Nolan. He has Grogan, the Chief of Police, in his pocket. Look! That's Grogan peeking out of Nolan's coat-tails.'

I met a woman who owned a night-club in Las Vegas called 'The Igloo'. She told me she was a Eskimo.

'You've got a funny accent for an Eskimo,' I said.

'Well,' she said, 'you've heard of Nanook of the North. Well, I'm Eskimo Nell from way down south, you-all. I had a sister Florrie. She was known as Ice-Floe, but things got tough. We had a deep depression over Iceland and there was a wage freeze. Ice-Floe drifted way down south and disappeared. I married an Eskimo called Esky Moe Iceberg, and we lived just north of the North Pole. He was a movie actor and had played 007 Centigrade in the movie *Coldfinger*.

'We first met at an ice-rink in the Street of a Thousand Ice-holes by the sign of the Freezing Mitt. I was wearing the latest Eskimo fashion at the time. Cold pants. The temperature was forty below and not much more above. It was cold. Esky Moe told me it was love at first sight. "Get a load of that dame!" he had said to himself. "What a pair of nostrils! Like pools of pitch in the snow!"

'I tell you, Tommy,' said Eskimo Nell, 'It was a cold romance. Moe seized me in a freezing embrace and crushed me to him like ice. He said, "Your nose is so wonderful. So hard, so cold." I could feel his freezing breath in my face. We rubbed noses with a freezing passion. I agreed to marry him and we sealed it with a sniff.

'Moe took me to see his uncle. He was a big shot. He was on the cold line to Moscow when we walked in. He was actually an Eskimo rajah who had patented a sauce made from ice. It was a chilly sauce. His name was Birra Jam which means Big Jim. He was called B. Jam for short. He owned a frozen foods factory and advertised a lot on ETV (Eskimo Television).

'Moe and I were married and we bought our own igloo.

That's an icicle built for two. It had everything as far as convenience was concerned. You could get to it on the Arctic Circle or the Northern Line, change at Whitechapel. We were proud of our home. We decided to make a house cooling and invite all our friends for drinks and dinner.

'I told Moe to get the sledge from the garage and nip down to the supermarket. It was a very cold nip. I told him to pick up a penguin, just imported from the South Pole and, maybe, lampoon a whale or two on the way. We would have a whale of a time. I also reminded him to get some cleaning materials – Eskimo Snow and a carton of Cold Automatic.

'Moe put on his ice-cap and went to get the sledge from the garage. It wouldn't start. Moe had to get some anti-freeze to unfreeze the dog from the lamp-post. Moe finally drove off singing, "Sledge dogs and Eskimos go out in the midnight sun."

'All the big shots of the Eskimo community turned up at the house cooling. There were reporters from the *Midnight Sun* and the *Freezing News*, lots of people from ETV including Dan-Dan the Weatherman. He looked nervous but was putting up a cold front. Felix Oneupski, the Polish explorer, was there. He told me his brother was exploring the South Pole. The fact that they were both explorers and were both up the pole was all they had in common. Actually they were Poles apart.

'We served snowballs and frozen Daiquiris for drinks. We ran out of ice. I chopped a few cubes from the walls. For dinner, we had blubber paté, followed by deep-frozen penguin. Next we had glacier mince, served with ice chips and greens from Greenland. For dessert, we had chocolate moose, complete with antlers, with a delicious sauce of pink candles. There was iced coffee, after which we chatted and sucked frozen peas. The men drank brandy and smoked fish. The party was a great success.

'And so life went on,' said Eskimo Nell. 'Moe pottered

26

about the igloo and thawed logs for the fire in the backyard. We had our snow flakes and whale juice for breakfast in the morning. We kept pets: a polar bear and an arctic fox. Both appeared on ETV in the glacier mint commercial. It brought us in a few extra bucks. We gave parties and discussed art, politics, but tried to avoid talking about the weather. You had only to mention in company that the weather was cold and some patriotic Eskimo would take the cue.

'"Cold? Did you say cold?"' he would shout and everyone felt obliged to freeze to attention and sing the Eskimo National Anthem, "The Snow-spangled Banner."

'I will now sing it for you, Tommy!' said Eskimo Nell.

I was touched. I must have been as I listened to her plaintive wail. I forgot the song but remember the touching.

Eskimo Nell paused to chip an icicle from her eye before she carried on. 'I had a boy we called Horatio. He was known to one and all as Horatio, Nell's son. Moe's ambition was for him to be an admiral in the Eskimo Navy. Not much of a future, I thought, to be an admiral of a fleet of canoes. However, Horatio grew up and changed his name to Hornblower. He went off to Hollywood to look for Gregory Peck.

'Life was wonderful for a time, but of course, it could not last. Eventually our love began to grow warm and Moe took to giving me melting glances. This, as you know, is not so hot for an Eskimo. So, finally, I told him to go paddle his own canoe. We rubbed noses for the last time and I left him with his nose well out of joint.

'Sometimes, when I get lonesome, I sleep in the deep freeze and dream about Esky Moe Iceberg.'

This, then, was the sad ballad of Eskimo Nell. I shed a tear or two and said how sorry I was.

'Don't be,' said Nell. 'Fellas leave me cold. They cut no ice with me nowadays.'

I went home and turned the central heating full up.

While I was in the States I was asked to do a Western film for TV I've always been crazy about Westerns. I read all the Western comics as a kid – Tom Mix, Rex Ritter, Rocky Lane and Roy Rogers. So when it comes to Westerns I know what I'm talking about.

We went on location way out West to a town called Sleepy Hollow. The windows were yawning, and the doors had dropped off. The only sign of life was some centipedes and these were on their last legs. I went into a store and bought one of the new ten-litre hats. Then I went up Boot Hill for some boots.

I walked across the road to the saloon. There was Granny Croakley, Wild Bill Hiccup and Daniel Goon. I recognised them all.

I made my first mistake when the bartender asked me what I wanted. I said I wanted a couple of shots and held up a couple of fingers. Granny Croakley, who had been dozing, woke up and shouted 'Draw!' She fired two shots and I almost lost two fingers. But I drew her a quick sketch.

Wild Bill Hiccup made for his gun. He was quick on the trigger and slow on the draw. He fired before he had unholstered his pistol. He shot himself in the foot. He was hopping mad. He threw a gun at me. It hit me on the left ear. He was a gunslinger. Daniel Goon pointed a gun at me but he couldn't fire. I had put my finger over the hole.

The Clapham Kid walked in. He had a Colt 45 in one hand and a hot 45 in the other. 'How do you like it?' he said. 'Hot or colt?'

I took off. Outside in the street, I saw a cowboy with a

horse across his shoulders. He glared at me.

'What's wrong, amigo?' he shouted. 'Haven't you ever seen a cowboy carrying a colt before?'

I went off to find the Indian village. I knew I was getting near it. I could hear the dogs pow-wowing. I met the Red Indian Chief.

'Me, Tommy Cooper,' I said. 'Me come in peace.'

'Me Tommy Hawk,' he answered. 'Soon you go in pieces.'

I offered to smoke the pipe of peace with him.

'Pipe of peace?' he said. 'Me no smokum. Medicine man, he say pipe bad for health. So up your pipe. I give you cigar.'

He was a cigar store Indian. He said: 'White man speak with forked tongue.' I said 'I'm sorry, but I was eating peas and my fork slipped.' It was a slip of the tongue and I slipped away on it.

There was a big tepee. It had been thatched with scalps. It was a wigwam. It had a sign. It was an Indian sign. It said 'The Bombay Restaurant'. There was an Indian outside wearing a turban with a feather. It was a feather in his cap. He was singing 'Curry me back to ol' Virginny.' He told me that the wigwam was the new Indian restaurant and did I want to make an Indian Reservation. He said his name was Smith, alias Kid Curry. He used to be in a TV comedy series made for Sunday morning viewers. It was called the *Curry On* series. In one show he had played the part of a cowboy and had been showered with curry pies. It was called *Curry on, Cowboy!* He said he had a partner. His name was Jim Bhowani and he was from up the junction. He was a sacred cowboy and had left England because the taxman was milking him.

There were a couple of Indian scouts hanging about with their scoutmaster. They were waiting to take stones out of horses' hooves with their scout knives. They tried to flog me a horse. They said it was the finest horse in the West. It was a sea-horse. It was a Western Super-Mare.

5

Cooper on Show

I WAS ONCE DOING a road-show and a policeman told me to move on. We brought the show to London. The timing was bad. We arrived just after the Lord Mayor's show.

I had just taken my exam for the Magic Circle. I was in the Secret Six. It's so secret I don't even know who the other five are. One of the tricks I had to perform was with marked cards. I nearly failed. My marks weren't high enough.

In the show we had a disc jockey. He was always in a spin and wandering off the track. He was badly handicapped. He used to walk about in jockey shorts and a peaked cap.

The stage of the theatre was small. On the opening night I stood in the centre of the stage to take a curtain call. I threw out my arms. I knocked out the teeth of the manager standing in the wings on one side, and dented the nose of an electrician standing in the wings on the other.

I was in band shows, you know. I once played in a brass band. I was a drummer. I was drummed out for knocking holes in the drums. One night, when we were playing in Southport, I went to the theatre for rehearsals. I met another drummer, Tim Panny. He was trying to drum up some business. He had been fired from his last job for making tea and boiling the water in the kettle-drum. Syd, the cornet player, was sucking a cornet. It was an ice-cream cornet. Mike the trumpet player was blowing his own trumpet. He was playing 'Trump, trump, trump along the Highway!' I was on the harp, but I was told by the conductor not to harp on it. I should have been on the piano but I had left my keys in the car. We were all on the fiddle.

Our conductor liked fast music. He was a lightning conductor. He sent me out to buy a few balls of string for our string quartet. They were going for a 'Holiday in Strings'. I was wearing a string vest for the occasion.

I had a pain in the back of my head, trying to duck the trombone player, a pain in the ear from the bass baritone, and a pain in the neck from one and all.

I was doing a summer season in Torquay. There was a girl on the bill married to a man called Art. She told me it was her third husband called Art. She was an Art lover.

Torquay is a very nice town, you know. I used to go to a tea-shop called 'The Doll's House'. It was run by two brothers. They were known as the Dolly Sisters. They were always ready to scratch your eyes out. One asked me if I knew what good clean fun was.

'I give up,' I said. 'What good is it?'

Claudia, his name was Claudia but everyone called him 'Claude, dear', was very upset. He poured tea in my lap.

'Thanks,' I said, real sarcastic.

I went to a fish bar. It was a very popular place. I ate a nice piece of fivepenny skate. It was a cheapskate. The orchestra was playing a selection from *Kiss Me Skate*.

Sometimes I went to a café on the front. The Boss

stood at the door rapidly counting the people coming in for lunch. He was a quick lunch counter. His nephew was the manager. He was a bad manager. The clients used to pinch knives, forks, spoons, chairs and suchlike. He took no notice. He buried his head in the sand. He was ostrichised by his uncle.

I once called him over to my table.

'These sausages are funny,' I said. 'One end is meat, the other end is bread.'

'I'm sorry,' he said. 'That's the way the cookie crumbles. In these days of inflation, it's hard to make both ends meat.'

And talking about that, I went into an expensive restaurant in Bond Street once. I saw Sir Ali Baba, the Arabian Knight, ordering a salt-beef sandwich there.

'Make it lean!' he ordered.

'Yessir!' said the waiter. 'To the left or to the right?'

I asked the waiter to bring me a menu.

'Look here,' I said. 'It says, "Hot Chicken Soap with Bitter Beans."'

'All right,' he said. 'So that's what it says. So what you see is misprints. It happens all the time. Our printer is an old dog. Don't get so excited.'

'What do you mean, your printer is an old dog?' I asked.

'I mean,' said the waiter, 'he's an old type-setter.'

He laughed himself into a knot. Later I complained that the chopped fish wasn't well-chopped.

'Look,' said the waiter, 'if you had let us know you were coming, we could have given it a few extra karate chops, especially for you.'

I stuffed a couple of salt-beef sandwiches into my back pocket and went out. I went across the road to Bald Ben's barber shop. His speciality is a scalp massage with bay rum. He's known as Ben, the Rum Baba.

While I was there a man came in.

'I want a haircut,' he said.

'Yessir!' said Ben. 'Which one? You've got two.'

'All right,' said the man, 'cut them both – but mind, not too short.'

After that I took a taxi to see my consultant. My consultant refused to see it. He said he wasn't a taxi consultant. He said he wasn't well and had been to see a consultant himself. The consultant had demanded twenty pounds, until he reminded him he was on his panel.

'Now what's your trouble?' he asked.

'I've got a sore throat,' I said.

'Right, Mr Cooper,' he said, 'poke out your tongue.'

I poked out my tongue.

'Poke it out further,' he said.

'How can I?' I asked. 'It's fastened at the other end.'

'Pity,' replied the doctor. 'Well, stop eating sweets. They're bad for you. Try eating carrots instead.'

'I would look silly sitting in a train sucking a carrot instead of a lollipop.'

'Oh, I don't know that it would make all that difference,' he said. 'Well, there are a couple of things you must give up, but you can sing all you want.'

Oh, really? I thought.

'You've got tonsillitis, I'll give you a bottle of medicine. Take a spoonful three times a day.'

'Level or heaped?' I enquired.

'Shredded,' he shouted.

'By the way,' I said, 'can you do a hair transplant?'

'We're fresh out of hares,' was the reply, 'but I can do you a rabbit transplant, that is, if I had a rabbit.'

I pulled one out of a hat.

I was sent to hospital and I had my tonsils out. Just like that!

After the operation I went for a short holiday in Spain to recuperate. Yuk! Yuk! We went to the Costa del Sol.

I used to think Costa del Sol was Spanish for the price of fish.

You need to have your wits about when travelling abroad. I always take my wits with me. First thing I pack is my wits. My wife always reminds me to pack my own wits and pieces. I always say you can't beat a nice pair of wits.

I needed my wits about me all right. One day I went to a Spanish market to buy some oranges. The *señorita* wanted twenty pesetas for Seville oranges. I said I didn't mind if they were unseville for ten.

There were lots of people standing around selling small packages. They were package dealers. I bought a package. I was told it was an autographed souvenir of Lolita, the great Spanish peeler. I opened it. It was a signed onion.

Lolita was actually a flamenco dancer. She was well reared. She looked good in front too. Pound for pound she wanted some beating. One night, when she was dancing at the night club, she stamped her foot and it went through the floor. Everyone shouted *Olé!* There was a sudden disturbance. It was Mad Maria from Marylebone singing 'Ave Maria'.

She was strumming a guitar with one foot and dancing a fandango with the other. She started doing a fan dance. You could feel the air was electric. She was using an electric fan. There was a sudden hush. A puppy whimpered. It was a hush puppy. She started singing a haunting refrain. It was called 'Come in now, the ghost is clear'. I held my breath. It made my hands hot. Even Lolita was moved. The manager moved her to the back of the hall. She had taken a back seat.

Mad Maria suddenly stopped singing and began to recite an old Spanish love poem. It was called, 'Listen to me while I tell you of the blighter who blighted my life.' Immediately all the Spanish waiters took off and haven't been seen till this day. That is, except for one, I met a year or two later. He was a waiter in a Chinese restaurant in Chorlton-cum-Hardy.

'Aha,' he sighed. 'I shed a tear for the black haired Maria.'

He dropped a Spanish Egg Fu Yung into my lap and danced off clicking his castanets.

When I got back from Spain I had to go to Bristol. I was driving up the M4 when I spotted a man trudging along the hard shoulder. I recognised him immediately. It was Mad Ken from Kensington. He was singing, 'D'ye Ken John Peel', and peeling an orange.

He was wearing his double-breasted boots with hammer toe-caps and fur-lined boot laces, black tights, a potato jacket and a cup tie. He looked very elegant. He was wheeling a barrow. It was full of wheels. It was a wheelbarrow.

I stopped and said, 'Hello Ken. What are you on?'

'I'm on my way to Bath,' he said.

'You're going the wrong way,' I pointed out.

'I know I am. I'm not daft,' he said. 'I'm just going back for my rubber duck.'

He upped his barrow and made off doing a fast tango along the fast lane. I drove on.

Later, I stopped at a pub, way out in the country, for a

fork lunch. I ate a dozen forks. When I came out to the car park, my car had gone. There was a note nailed to a traffic warden. It just said 'Sorry, I couldn't wait.' I had no option. I had to go to the station to catch a train. I asked the stationmaster about the times of the trains. He was an old buffer. In the waiting room I found a couple of sleepers. On the wall was a time-table. It was dated 1924.

To while away the time until the train to Bristol arrived, I woke up the sleepers and offered to show them a few card tricks.

'Has anyone got a pack of cards?' I asked.

'Here,' said one. 'Take this giant family pack – two pence off. Or this one with fifty eight cards – a special six card bonus offer.' He was a supermarket salesman.

'No,' said the other man. 'Take my cards. They're stamped up to date. I won't be needing them. I just got eight draws.'

The train eventually arrived on time, but I wasn't there. I had got steamed up and made tracks out of the place the month before.

6

Cooper Capers

ONCE I WAS ASKED to do a show called *The Garden of Allah*. It was at the Winter Gardens in Blackpool. A man called Fred was the gardener. I was playing the part of a rake. It was the first time I met Fred, although I had come across him many times before.

'What's that hair on the top of your ears, Fred?' I asked him.

'Earwigs, Tommy,' he said. 'They keep my ears warm.'

'Y'know, Tommy,' he went on, 'I've just come from doing Madison Square Garden, but I haven't always been in gardens, y'know. Oh-ho-no, Tommy! I was a bit of an actor. I got bit parts. The parts got blooming bigger. Then it was roses all the way to the Floral Hall, Scarborough, Tommy.'

'Come to see me at home, Tommy,' said Fred. 'I grow tobacco plants. I'll pick you a nice fresh cigar.'

Fred found a leek in his ear and started to chew it.

'By the way, Tommy,' he said. 'Do you know what you get if you cross melon with cauliflower?'

'You get melancholy,' I said.

'You're a proper seed card, Tommy,' said Fred. 'Nobody's ever going to lead you up the old garden path. Well, cheerio, Tommy. Cheerio everybody.'

Fred disappeared behind a compost heap.

I played in panto. I was in Humpty Dumpty but it got a bit too windy when the wall I sat on turned out to be made of breeze blocks. I played Puss-in-Boots until I got too big for my boots. I also played the cat in *Dick Whittington*. I got the sack for staying out all night on the tiles. I got a part in *Red Riding Hood* because I could ride. I was offered two parts in *Cinderella*, as both the ugly sisters. I played Bo Peep in a revue called *Peep Show*. Everyone called me 'Peeping Tom'.

In 1967 I was in a movie called *The Plank*, with Eric Sykes. It was a toss-up to see who would play the part of the plank. The producer said we were both thick enough.

I played the Moss Empires even before the Rolling Stones had started to gather Moss. I played the Manchester Opera House, though, personally, I never thought opera was anything to sing about.

I worked a summer season in Torquay. I was in a play. It was about a horse. It was a horse-play. I had a lot of horse-sense in those days.

At our digs there were some very funny people. There was a movie actor who acted in horror movies. His name was Frank N. Stein. He said he had been made for the part. His mother was an old bat, his father was an old creep.

Then there was an old man who played Mother Goose. He was fired for taking a gander where he shouldn't. His name was Miller. He had a millstone round his neck. It was his wife, Millie.

There was a short man with a flat head, we called him Shortstuff. In the crowded local, people would often draw up a chair to him and put their pint and a packet of crisps on his head, then look around for an ashtray.

He told me he specialised in playing short plays.

'The last theatre I played in,' he said, 'was dead. You could tell by the way it had been laid out. Even the lease had expired.'

Talking of supermarkets, I get tired of shopping with my wife. She says I'm very understanding though. I'm always standing under her feet. She takes me around the supermarket in one of those trolleys. One day at the checkout they thought I was something on offer. A kid pointed at me and started howling. He told his Mum that he wanted one of those. My wife said he could have me.

I used to spend a lot of time at the broadcasting studios. One day I got an arrow right through my ear. The Archers were rehearsing next door. My producer was a very wealthy man. He was the first man ever to wear a mohair wig to match his suit.

I met a showbiz impressario, he asked me if I knew the five card trick. I said I did.

'Well,' he said, 'for me, do it with three.'

At that moment there was a commotion outside his office. It was Mad Lew from Lewisham. He was trying to make an impression by singing 'Lew-Lew's back in Town'.

'I used to be a baritone', said Lew, 'but ever since I had all my teeth out, I've been singing falsetto. All the same, people are beginning to talk.'

I went to a party given by a famous cook. She was in the kitchen singing, 'If I knew you were coming I'd have baked a cake', and demonstrating how to boil an egg. She told me the secret of being a classy cook.

'Always used refined sugar,' she said, 'and never use common salt.'

My agent came in then, smiling. He told me he had booked me for a big TV commercial. I was to do the sound effects.

I left and went down the tube to get from Oxford Street to Shepherds Bush. Phew! What a walk. I should have waited for the train.

I felt someone dogging my footsteps. It was a dog. He invited me to join him for a meal at the Kennel Club. I wasn't sure, but I went.

He told me about two dogs who had a night out and were hounded from pillar to post. Finally, one stood on the kerb and said to his mate, 'Time to go. Let's have one for the road.' I gave a couple of te-hes.

We went into the dining-room at the club. The waiters and waitresses seemed to be down in the mouth, more than somewhat. They needed perking up.

'I'll teach you a trick that will make you the life and soul of the party,' I said to our waiter. 'All you have to do is take a spoon and throw it into the air. While it is falling, make a quick cup of tea, then catch the spoon in the cup, without stirring. If the trick doesn't go down too well, you'll find that the tea will.'

The waiter, who looked like a bloodhound, didn't seem amused. I asked him to send over the wine waiter. A waiter trotted up to our table.

'Are you the wine waiter?' I asked.

'Yes,' he said.

'Well', I said, 'let's hear you whine!'

He snapped at me.

The waiter brought us a dog-eared menu. He sat back on his haunches and waited.

'I'll start with the pate, mate', I said.

'It's pronounced *paté*', he said.

'All right,' I said, 'I'll have the *paté*, *maté*.

He knew he had a customer today.

'Next,' I said, 'I'll have the tickled beef.'

'You mean pickled beef,' he said, smiling.

'It says "tickled beef" on the menu,' I pointed out.

'I see, sir,' he said. 'It's a misprint. The T should be P.'

'Look!' I said, 'T or P, I don't care how it's pickled. Fetch it! I'm hungry!'

'And what would you like with it?' the waiter said, coldly. 'May I suggest beans? We have a selection. We have Chinese beans that sprout, Mexican beans that jump and other beans that are just scarlet runners. We have broad beans and narrow beans. Or perhaps you would be interested in our Harry Knott. He's a French bean.'

'I can see you are full of beans yourself,' I said.

The Mad Parson from Parson's Green was there. I hadn't seen him for years. He was seated at the next table, wearing a hang-dog expression and a cup he had won at Crufts when he had been mistaken for a St. Bernard. It was hanging from his dog-collar, instead of a barrel.

He was drinking beer and munching dog-biscuits. They reminded me of my mother's biscuits and I felt a lump in my throat. He must have drunk a lot of beer. The next thing, he tried to blow the foam off a mad dog. He glanced at his dog-watch and whistled. He hurried off, pausing in the doorway to wave a cheery leg at us, and barking his shin.

My companion shook his head sadly.

'I'm afraid that poor man is going to the dogs,' he said. 'They're racing at the White City Stadium.'

The waiter brought our coffee. I said it tasted like mud.

'I'm not surprised, sir,' he said, 'it was ground this morning.'

'I thought so,' I said. 'I can see it's been through the mill.'

'Bow! Wow!' barked the waiter, and bit my leg.

43

7

Chinese Crackers

ONCE I APPEARED in cabaret at the Mandarin Hotel in Hong Kong. It was great. I did the Chinese rope trick. It's like the Indian rope trick, only you do it sideways. There was also a Chinese comedian called Chi Ken, the Chinese wise-cracker. He had known all the Chinese big shots – Mousy Tongue, Shanghai Jack and Chew and Lie. He had even visited the Chinese Premier at his country home, Chinese Chequers.

I was suffering from an ingrowing corn plaster and Chi Ken sent me to see his own doctor. His name was Fu Man Chu. He wasn't what he was cracked up to be. He told me I needed to build up my strength. I said I would take a job in a dyers and cleaners doing press-ups. I went back to the hotel and picked up a couple of bar belles. I suddenly remembered that on the latest tax forms, they ask if you can lift a sack of potatoes. If you say yes, they tax your strength. I decided not to bother.

I went to see a Chinese movie. It started at the end and finished at the beginning. It was about a young Chinese couple, Fa Tsu and Wei Pi who had got together and were trying to drift apart. It was called *The Chinese Disconnection*.

I went to a famous floating restaurant in Hong Kong. I heard someone ask for lasagne.

'Lasagne in a Chinese restaurant?' I asked a waiter.

'Yessir,' he said. 'We try to please our Irish clientele.'

There was one man there who was a Kung Fu expert.

He didn't use chopsticks. He used choppers. He had chops with everything.

I am an expert on Chinese food myself. I ordered a double portion of fifty-two, a double portion of seventy-six and a portion of sixty-three. I complained there wasn't enough number nine in the seventy-six. The manager said he would speak to the chef, Wun Ten, who had been at sixes and sevens all day.

An American asked for Kung Fu instead of egg fu yung and was nearly kicked to death. For dessert I ordered some Lie Cheese and biscuits.

While I was waiting, a queer-looking man came in. He had a high, domed head and was wearing tights and a frock-coat. He was shown to one of the best tables in the restaurant.

'Who is that man with the prominent seat?' I asked a waiter.

'Why!' said the waiter, 'that is Rick Shaw known to one and all as the Great (Max) Wall of China. He's the star of the Chinese TV show, *Wu do you do?*'

At that moment there was a sudden disturbance. It was Mad Ching from Chingford chinging a Chinese love chong.

I went back to the Mandarin Hotel, and sat quietly at the back of the bar. I was doing a Chinese crossword puzzle which I found very difficult especially as I don't know Chinese.

I did four across and five down but was stuck at number six up, when I heard a row start at the next table. It was Hi-Lo and Lo-Hi, a couple of Chinese contortionists. They were playing Pa-jongh which is like Ma-jongh except you keep saying, 'How's your father?' They were each accusing the other of twisting. Hi-Lo did a quick handstand on Lo-Hi's head. This threw Lo-Hi off balance. He stalked off in a huff, very dignified and with Hi-Lo still perched on his head. He was headstrong.

Nobody took much notice as such goings on were common in Hong Kong.

On the Wai Chai waterfront I met a man, Sam Pan, the old Chinese boatman. He was a junkman.

I asked him where I could find a Chinese laundry. He took me to a place called 'The Washeteria of the Fifth Happiness'. It turned out to be a front for a gambling den, run by a chap named Ho-Ho. I was taken to the cleaners and I lost my shirt.

I had my eye on one of the tables. I gave it to a sloe-eyed maiden. A quick-eyed fellow with her threw me a dirty look. It hit me hard. I was hurt. I turned a blind eye. I wasn't looking for an eyeball to eyeball confrontation.

I recognised Wo Fat the spymaster from *Hawaii Five O*. He was with his brother, Fat-Fat. He was called Fat-Fat because not only was he fat, he was double fat.

They were talking to a beautiful red-headed Chinese girl, known as Chinese Ginger.

Po Lo, a Chinese TV personality who was sucking holes out of mints, told me that the girl was a spy. He told me how she had outwitted Double Seven O, the Chinese quadruple agent.

Double Seven O had been suffering from a deep depression due to the weather and a night out with Fan Tan the Chinese fan-dancer. He was wearing braces to keep his chin up.

He was taken by surprise when Chinese Ginger broke into his apartment. He almost busted his braces. His jaw dropped and his voice broke. She pointed a finger at him. It was a trigger finger. It was a finger of scorn.

'What is the meaning of this?' he asked in a broken voice.

'This is a stick-up!' she said, and she started pasting him. She then strapped him to a bed-post. She was a strapping girl. She started to search the room. There was a tallboy in the corner. She gave him a good pasting too. She liked to keep everyone well pasted.

She removed something from the wall and trod on it. It was a bug.

'This place has been bugged,' she said.

She soon found the code she was looking for. It was the Hei Wei Code. It was hidden in the soda cypher in the cocktail cabinet.

'Now,' she said, 'I want your contacts.'

'They're over there in my glasses-case with my spy-glasses,' said Double Seven O.

'Where is the waitress, Sue, today?' I asked.

'She in hospital,' said Chang. 'Velly bad. Chef all time he chop Suey. He in police-station. Boss, he away for weekend. Big sporting man. Take guns, go on bamboo shoot. Now, sir, you try the fifty-seven. It is new variety. Make up mind quick. I gotta go outside, water the chestnuts.'

'By the way,' I asked, 'who is that man over there with the Kung Fu moustache?'

'Not moustache,' said Chang. 'That man eating soft noodles.'

'In that case,' I replied, 'I'll have twenty-five to thirty-one for starters.'

Chang was impressed with my handling of figures. He asked me to look after the accounts for his new company, Chong (Year of the Dragon) Limited. He had gone bankrupt last Christmas.

As he scuttled off to find the papers I took out my pocket calculator. I need all the help I can get when I'm ordering the main course.

48

'Well, that's it!' said Chinese Ginger. 'Now I've got to silence you.'

She slipped the silencer off her pistol and put it over his head. It was a tight fit.

She took out a camera. It was made of liquorice. It was a candy camera. Her father had been a photographer. She was well developed and had a good photo-finish. She took a quick picture of Double Seven O. She gave him a farewell kiss.

'Y'know,' he said, 'your kisses taste of the Orient.'

'I'm not surprised,' she said. 'I've just been eating Chinese Tai Kwai, which, translated into English, means food.'

She went out singing, 'Water pitcher, water pitcher, Hi tiddly um tum-tum-tum! Keep it in your family . . .'

The story was interrupted by a sudden disturbance. It was the Mad Baker, Lew Baker from Bakerloo. He was throwing ticker tapes. Po Lo went outside and told him to go underground again. Lew said, 'That's the yeast I can do.' He borrowed some dough and we never saw him again.

Back at the hotel we went down to the cabaret to see Fan Tan, the Chinese Fan Dancer. What a performance! She took off everything. In the end, she was left with a single feather. It was a feather in her cup. Everyone gave her the 'Chinese cheer'. It is a raspberry with a Chinese flavour.

Next there was a Chinese juggler juggling with Chinese clubs. These are the same as Indian clubs except that you throw them back to front. One flew out of his hands. It was a flying club. I did my act next. I sawed a Chinaman in half. There was a slight hitch. When I made him reappear the bottom half was back to front. Watching the show was the famous Chinese actor Tommy Kor Tnee, he was in that movie, *The Loneliness of a Side-distance Runner.*

I went shopping for souvenirs. I got hold of a Chinese backscratcher, but my wife wouldn't let me bring her home. When I did get home from Hong Kong, I wrote a poem. It was in Chinese, but I could never translate it.

I had acquired the taste for Chinese food some years ago, and used to lunch regularly at a restaurant in Charing Cross Road. Well, although I'm somewhat of an expert on China, my uncle used to have a china stall in Portobello Road, I knew little Chinese. In fact the only other Chinese I knew was another poem, I learnt it from the boys at school. It was recited very rapidly, and I forgot it very rapidly. It may have been the Chinese version of Gunga Din.

This restaurant was a home from home for me. I knew all the staff. They didn't all look alike to me. We treated each other familiarly. One day I took my usual table and the manager asked me where I was taking it.

Chong, the cheeky Chinese waiter greeted me.

'Hello, me old China,' he said.

'For starters,' I said, 'I can do without your sweet and sour sauce.'

'Velly good joke, Mr Clooper,' he answered, 'it real spare-rib tickler. You not so daft in the noodles.'

THERE WILL NOW BE A SHORT
INTERMISSION . . .

Trickery Nook

ANYONE CAN BE the life and soul of a party if they can do a few baffling tricks. The tricks I'm going to tell you about are very baffling. They even baffle me.

Now, when doing tricks make sure your audience is awake, but not too wide awake or you might get one of those know-it-all Charlies giving the game away. Do a bit of the old patter; the old friendly chatter. It helps take people's minds off exactly how you are doing what. Wave a bamboo cane about. It will bamboozle your audience. Do a bit of what they call 'business' in the business. A little horseplay, you know: I saw this poor little horse. It was starving. It had no fodder. What is worse, it had no modder.

Now here's an easy trick. It usually makes a big impression. It's a variation of the old sawing a lady in half bit. So you'll need a saw. Place your hand on a table and tell your audience you are going to saw off a finger. Saw off a finger. Then hold up your hand and show you still have five fingers. *Wait! As you were! Hang about!* I should have mentioned that to do this trick successfully you need to be six fingered to start with.

Here's another finger trick. It's called the ink finger trick. You take a small glass of water. Ask anyone to stir it with a finger. Whoever does it will get a wet finger. That's all. Now you hold up a finger. Make sure you don't stick up two. Stir the water with the finger and what happens? It will turn to ink. Your audience will fall about.

How is this trick done? You may well ask. I'll tell you. You prepare the water by adding a couple of drops of tincture iodine so that it barely discolours the water. Make a paste of some corn or potato starch, enough to put under your fingernail, and let it dry. Make sure that's the finger you put in the water. I showed this trick to my mum. She said, 'That's nothing. When you were a kid I used to shove you in the bath and we would get a whole bath full of ink.'

Here's a great trick shown to me by The Great Dan, the underground man. Make a simple line drawing of a girl's head on a piece of white paper. Paint her cheeks with a solution of phenolphthalein. This is a big word. Nobody knows how to spell it, not even the Mad Brain of Britain, but you can get the stuff at the chemists. Let the picture dry. The solution is then colourless. Take two jars of fishpaste. Eat the paste and after you've recovered, wash out the jars. Fill one with ordinary household ammonia and the other with plain tap water. Now you are ready.

Hold up the picture and ask a member of the audience to come forward and place a glass of water to the girl's lips. When he does, nothing happens. When you do this, the girl's cheeks turn red. Take away your glass and her cheeks become normal. Hold the glass to her face again and she blushes. Make sure the glass you use is the one with the ammonia. You don't have to draw a girl's face for this trick. Draw a turnip you can turn into a beetroot, or anything else you can think of, like a nose on a face. The mind boggles with ideas.

I came into the studio one day and found our Mrs Mop bashing the producer's desk with a cane.

'What's the table done to you?' I asked.

'Nothing,' she said, 'but the producer said I could clean it with whacks.'

I thought it was a good trick, but how it cleans a desk baffles me.

Here's a trick you could try out in a pub, but choose your audience carefully or you could wind up with a broken arm.

Put one fist on top of another and challenge anyone to separate them. In fact, it's almost impossible to pull them apart. After one or two people have had a go, say that you can do it to anybody who thinks you can't. Now instead of pulling at the fists, extend the forefingers on each hand and with a swift movement strike the top fist with your left finger to the right, and the bottom fist with your right finger to the left. That'll do the trick all right. Now you pause for admiration and drink all the beer everyone has bought for you.

'Right,' you say 'I've shown you how it is done, but you can't do that to me.'

Someone is sure to want to have a go but he won't budge your fists. And why not? Simple. You work a flanker. You place one fist over the other, but grip your bottom thumb as shown in the sketch. Of course, don't make it obvious. I mean if anybody gets hurt, you don't want it to be you.

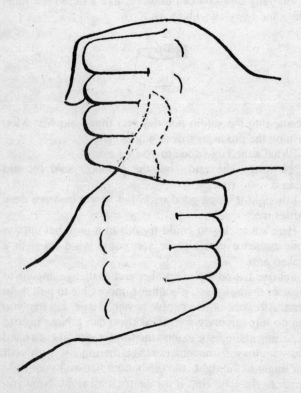

We had a man in the office once. He ate the staples from the stapling machine. He said it was his staple diet. I knew

The Mad Parson from Parsons Green

I was told to pitch a tent. There was no pitch so I used creosote

This is me, Cooper the Trooper

Autumn leaves fall and are swept out of sight

It's just a question of finding the right magic words

The Mighty Cooperman

I used to spend a lot of time in the gym

Just like that!

a sailor who was always blubbering. He was a wailer. I merely mention this in passing while I'm thinking of my next trick. I knew a Chinese once. He struck himself with a chopper. He committed chop-sueycide. And talking of Chinese, here's a Chinese trick. I got it from an old opium smoker. It's called the Chinese smoke trick.

You take two glasses. Place one on top of the other (see

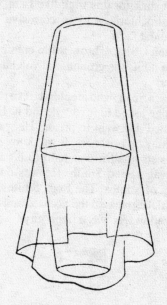

sketch) and cover quickly with a hand towel. Tell your audience you are going to blow smoke through the towel and into the glasses. Someone might say, 'So what?' Ignore him, her or it. Roll up a tissue and light it. Blow out the flame and as the paper smoulders blow the smoke towards the towel. Now say the magic phrase which is what the fiddler said to the flautist, 'Up your flute!' Remove the towel from the glasses. The glasses are full of smoke. Hold a glass in each hand and watch the faces of your audience as they watch your smoke.

How is it done? I'm not sure. Hang about. Yes. It's done like this. In one glass you put a drop of household ammonia. In the other a drop of hydrochloric acid. Keep the glasses covered until you use them. When the chemicals combine you get the smoke effect. You have to be quick and slick for this trick like I am, but a word of warning: hydrochloric acid is corrosive, so don't go throwing it about.

Here's a quick trick. Throw a 10p coin into the air and drill it before it hits the ground. All you have to do is use a 10p shooter.

There was a man who couldn't resist driving away cars. The judge asked him why he did it. He said he was just motorvated. He went to prison. He was put in a cell used for beating up prisoners. It was known as the hiding place. It was so small it was hard to do a good stretch. The judge was named Smith. He was one of the great Scottish clan of Smiths. The Loch Smiths. Once, during a murder trial, he released the accused and sent the whole jury to the gallows. It was a hung jury.

I was playing in a club in Scotland a few years ago. The cloakroom attendant had a long thin neck and narrow shoulders. She was a coathanger. This brings me to the trick with a coathanger.

Take the coathanger and hold it up to your audience. Remove your coat and trousers and hang them on the hanger. You are now hanging about without your coat and trousers. But never mind. Ask a member of the audience

58

to come forward and join you. Now for the tricky part. You say the magic words and lo and behold: *you* are fully dressed; *your* stooge is draped over the coathanger. This is a marvellous trick and I hope you have more luck with it than I've had. It's just a question of finding the right magic words. A word of warning. If the trick doesn't work you're apt to look a proper charlie.

Now what about the bottle trick, then? This is something to make you popular at any party. Pick on someone who looks like he has plenty of puff, but he sure he's smaller than you. Ask him to step forward and help you.

On the table, before you, you have two identical bottles. Each bottle has a cork or rubber stopper through which a piece of glass tubing extends, from a colourless liquid which half fills the bottle. You take one bottle and give your stooge the other. You give him a bit of the old patter about how you are going to test his powers of observation. He must do whatever you do.

Now you point out that you are holding the stopper down tightly. Then you blow down the tube hard. After each breath, hold the bottle up to your eye and look down at the stopper. Repeat until the liquid in the bottle turns milky.

'Right!' you say to your assistant. 'Let's see you do that, then.' Just like that. Make sure that he holds the stopper down, blows into the bottle hard, and then looks directly through the top of the glass tube (see previous page). Suddenly the liquid should spurt out of the tube right into his face. The result should be hilarious.

Here's how you prepare the trick. In one bottle you put a solution called limewater. It's harmless and colourless. In the other bottle you put plain tap water. Now, make sure you get the bottle with the limewater, and when you blow into the tube only pretend you are holding down the cork. Actually, be sure your stopper is loose. I might mention that I normally pick the wrong bottle, which I don't find funny. So watch it and you'll get top marks. But like I said, make sure you pick on a man smaller than you, just in case he can't take a joke.

60

I once worked for a toy factory. I was their top salesman. I sold thousands of tops. They were real money spinners.

A seagull flying over the sea caught a dolphin's eye.

'Sorry,' said the seagull, 'it was an accident.'

'It wasn't,' said his mate, 'you did it on porpoise.'

Patter, patter, patter. Patter, patter, patter.

Here's a great trick. Take half a dozen assorted spoons. Hold one up in your left hand or your right hand, or please yourself. Give it a melting glance. The handle will begin to bend. Look at the other spoons. You will find they too are bent. How is this fantastic trick done? You may well ask, and the person to ask is not me. I knew a copper who was bent and a diver who had the bends. But bending spoons always has me doubled up.

Ask a member of your audience to step forward. You show him a piece of blank paper. Patter, patter, patter. Patter, patter, patter. You say you will heat the paper over a lighted candle and his name will appear on it. If his name does appear on the candle everyone will be surprised, including me. But a name will appear on the paper.

The paper is prepared beforehand by writing a name on it like Bob, Bill or Jim, using a match dipped in milk or lemonade, and allowing it to dry. It dries colourless. This trick is great if the name you have written on the sheet really turns out to be the name of the person who comes forward. If not, grin and bear it. Just say, 'Well, what's in a name, anyway?' Patter, patter, patter. Patter, pitter, patter. How did that pitter get into the patter?

If you're simple, here's a simple trick. Simply arrange six tumblers in a row. Fill the first three with water. Leave the next three empty. Right! Now ask anyone to re-arrange them so that, starting with the first glass full, the glasses are full and empty alternately. But it must be done by moving one glass only. Just like that. Here's how simple it is. All you have to do is pour the water from glass tumbler two into glass number five and replace the emptied glass. For a variation of this trick, use beer instead of water.

If you're fond of figures, here's the magic number trick. I showed it to the Mad Brain of Britain and he was baffled. He couldn't figure it out. He fed it to a computer. It went mad. It burped and played a tune. The electricity board heard about it and bought it for a song.

Write the number 1089 on a piece of paper, put it into a sealed envelope. Getting a piece of paper into a sealed envelope isn't easy. Invite a brainy looking member of the audience to write down any three-figure number. Suppose he writes 954. Next ask him to write the reverse of the number. In this case it's 459; then subtract the smaller number from the larger, that is 954 less 459 which leaves 495. Now ask him to add this figure to the reverse figure. That is 495 plus 594. You open up the envelope and there is the answer. Try it with any three-figure number. It works everytime, if your guinea pigs get their sums right, that is.

Now back to the narrative . . . uh . . . story. Yes, where was I?

The story so far:

Jim, who had been engaged to Barbara before she met Jason, had been seeing a lot of Sheila – and Sheila herself, unknown to Jim, had gone to stay with Harry's friend, Joyce. Aunt Flo was expected any minute, but due to Jim and Barbara was now waiting until Harry made up his mind over Joyce. Sheila was busy rewriting some of Chopin's piano music when there was a knock on the door. Could it be Harry? And if so had he made up his mind about Joyce? Or was it Jim? Or Aunt Flo?

Now read on . . .

'Is Cooper writing a romantic novel?'
'Says he is.'
'Thought so. But it doesn't belong here, does it?'
'Well, it was in the typescript.'
'I know, but . . .'
'You want to get off at five-thirty?'
'Yes, I do.'
'Okay. We'll move onto the next page.'

8

Knights of Gladness

READING INTERSTS ME, you know. I've just finished reading a good book. It was called *Tolstoi* by Warren Peace. I was once in an Italian restaurant reading a book about Italian cooking. It was by the great Louis Pasta. I wanted to get the Italian atmosphere. The restaurant was as peaceful as an Italian vegetable market.

The proprietor was bald and his name was Gary. He was called Garibaldi. He was nibbling Garibaldi biscuits. He ate a lot of garlic and was in bad odour with his friends.

A man was sitting in the corner. I knew he was a musician. He was eating his pizza with a tuning fork.

In the kitchen, the chef and one of the waiters were singing 'O Sole Mio' as they ladled minestrone down each other's back. Another waiter was untying the knots in the spaghetti. I gave the waitress my order and she waddled away singing 'Chew, chew Bambino'. When she came back she dropped the ravioli down in front of me.

'Who put the meat in the ravioli?' I asked her.

'The chef, who else?' she said right back.

'Well, who took it out again?' I asked.

'You not be so funny,' she said, 'I not in the mood. My feet are killing me. My shoes pinch me at the bottom.'

'They must be Italian shoes,' I said.

'Oh!' she said. 'Now you make the insults. Well, I bring manager. You insult him.'

Garibaldi shuffled over to my table.

'What for you insult the lady for?' he said. 'All right. Maybe she not Sophia Loren. Maybe she not Claudia Cardinale. Maybe she not Gina Lollobrigida. She got something they not got, maybe.'

I was not in a position to answer that.

At that moment, there was a sudden disturbance. It was the Mad Roamer from Rome singing 'Roaming in the gloaming', and chucking Roman candles about.

Through the curtains, I saw the chef pour two gallons of milk into a tub, then ladle in great dollops of pasta.

'What's he doing?' I asked Garibaldi.

'What you think?' he said. 'He pastarising the milk'.
[PASTA-RISING THE MILK]

I said, 'I pass on the pasta' and I went out whistling, 'Arrive-derci Roman'.

As I said, I read a lot. I read about King Arthur and his Knights so I was pleased when I was asked to do a sketch for TV about King Arthur. It was about the days of old when Knights were bold and suchlike. I played the part of a rough Knight. I turned up late at the studio feeling very rough indeed, I was well suited for the part. I wore a new suit of pin-stripe armour with wire stitching. I carried a green shield I had got from trading stamps and a sword I had exchanged for old razor blades.

King Arthur was played by a small man who wore a double-breasted suit of armour with spiked knee-caps, and armour-plated glasses.

All the Knights were there. There was the White Knight. He was a square. He was a Knight of the square

66

table. There was Sir Loin, a big beefy man. He wanted a stake in our Knightly adventures. He was a specialist in Knight Operations. His uncle was the Baron of Beef in a steak-house in Barons Court. There was Sir Charge, from the tax office on his charger, and Sir Realist who looked a real mess.

Another Knight turned up as we were about to begin jousting. 'You've come joust in time', I said. He didn't answer. He couldn't speak English. He was French. I could tell by the plume in his helmet. It was 'La plume de ma tante'.

There was one man standing around looking a bit out of it. King Arthur asked him who he was. He said he was just an innocent bystander.

'Do you joust?' asked King Arthur.

'Joust a bit,' he answered.

'Are you handy with your arms?' said King Arthur.

'Well,' said the bystander, 'I'm not so handy with a sword, but I use a lance a lot.'

Arthur hit him across the shoulder with his sword.

'I hearby dub you, then,' he said, 'Sir Lancelot. Rise, Sir Lancelot!'

But the poor man couldn't stand up.

Arthur likes to have a good whack when he dubs. Now he had to dub his part.

In one jousting scene, a lance went right through my armour. It was lucky I had forgotten to put it on. I went to the blacksmith and told him the sleeves were too long. I was taken to the dungeons and put on the rack to have my arms stretched. Later we all went out looking for an inn for the night. It was an inn quest. We found an inn and on the staircase I saw a ghost. It was an inn spectre, a relation of Sir Charge. This inn was the in place. It was the local meading place. I ordered a mead and tonic.

One of the Knights stood a round. The rest of us just stood around. It was a one Knight stand. I met a strange Knight. We talked about tournaments. He looked to be an easy mark.

'Would you care for a joust?' I asked.

'Thanks very much,' he said, 'I'll have a tomato joust.'

A minstrel appeared. He was plucking his lute. We admired his pluck but his singing was rotten. We gave him the bird and told him to pluck that. We sent him to Coventry, and even Lady Godiva wouldn't talk to him. He had a rift in his lute.

I heard some sailors arrive. I could hear their bell-bottoms ringing. I asked one if he was an able seaman. He said he hadn't been able for a long time.

A Knight came in, his armour dripping wet. He was puffing and blowing. He was a wet and windy Knight. King Arthur had sent him to the castle with a message. It was a Knight errant. Then a herald arrived straight from the Angel at Islington. He was singing, 'Hark the Angel's herald sings'. He had a message from Parliament about an all Knight sitting. King Arthur called to me. He pointed to a group of pages standing at the bar.

'Stick this message on the front page,' he said.

I stuck it on his chest.

At that moment, the innkeeper shouted, 'Time gentlemen, please!'

There was just time to drink three or four more meads and a yard or two of ale before we were'turned out into the night.

It was pitch black, wet and windy. One of the men went ahead with a candle. It was a Knight light. Two of the sailors also went out like a light, so I carried them, one over each shoulder. I heard Sir George remark:

'God help the sailors on a Knight like this!'

There was a sudden disturbance. It was the Mad Knight from Knightsbridge singing, 'A Nightingale sang in Berkeley Square'. He turned to Baron Von Richthofen, the Red Knight of the Kaiser's Airforce and said:

'Shoot him down in flames.'

We rounded off the night with a feast. King Arthur wanted to know where the head of a round table was.

Saint George came in dragging an old dragon in drag. She was breathing fire. She said they were late because Saint George had lost the cast iron collar stud from his chain mail shirt, and his hose were wet. He had used his hose to water the horses.

I was in charge of the entertainment. A mystery entertainer did an act. He was wearing a hood. It was a Knighthood. It was me.

9

Short Story

A FRIEND OF MINE, Miles Short, is an inspector of weights and measures. He's a weight watcher. He was having a house built and invited me along to see the work in progress.

It was quite a site. It was between the Plenge Gasworks and the Tuppensoff Soap Factory. There was already an air about it.

When we arrived we found one workman groaning in agony. He was leaning on the wrong end of his shovel. His mate was busy with a pick. He was picking his teeth. Another man was going up a ladder carrying a hod of bricks. He missed a rung and dropped the lot. They landed on Paddy's head. He looked surprised.

'Begorrah!' he exclaimed. 'It's hailing, and not a cloud in the sky.'

Then there was a man filling a big pit with cement. I asked him what he was doing.

'I'm cementing relations,' he said. 'Well, just a few in-laws.'

We found the foreman chewing a concrete sandwich. He said he always liked to have something concrete. He asked us if we would like a drink. He poured out some vodka and went to a sack for some lime.

'I'm afraid we're having a spot of bother, Mr Short,' he said. 'We forgot to dig the foundations. Now we've got to put on our foundation garments and start again. Pity. We nearly had the house finished.'

A fellow came over to us. He spoke with a plum in his mouth. It was a plumber.

'I say, I say,' he said. 'Everyone else seems to be swinging the lead and I'm supposed to be the plumber.'

'And what about that creep, Fred?' he did continue. 'He's wearing the drainpipes again. Reckons they're coming back into fashion. How can I do the gutters while he's wearing the drainpipes? Tell me that. He must have been dragged up in the gutter. Speak to him, Harry. Harry, speak to him. He's always saying rude things to me.'

'All right, Gwen,' said Harry, 'don't fret. I'll talk to him.'

'Gwen? That's a funny name for a fella,' I said.

'Not really,' said Harry. 'His name is Gerald Gwen but he doesn't like to be called Gerald. He says it doesn't suit his image. Well, would you mind if I went off for a wash now? I'll just grab myself some sugar soap and a trowel. I'll be back before the next storey is finished.'

There was a sudden disturbance. It was the Mad Hod Carrier from Hoddesdon, singing, 'This breaking hod of mine keeps yearning, lover come back to me.'

The foreman yelled for him to stop. He just went on singing.

'I'm afraid,' said Harry, 'he's a little hod of hearing.'

The Mad Hod Carrier went on to give us a selection from the *Tiles of Hoffman*, and the *Cornice Green*.

One builder was speaking German. He was a jerry-builder. He broke into broken English.

'Vere ist der bricks? I had here zix' he said. 'Someone come and haf dem off-knocken. He thinks, maybe, I am dumber than the plumber. Dumkopf! I vill of him make der sausage meat. I will goosestep over his pimples. I vill his head stick in der sand right up to his feet.'

'All right! All right, already, Hans!' said Harry. 'Ash tongue! Ash tongue! I can see the bricks sticking out of your pants pocket. Who's a dumb cop, now, then?'

72

Harry turned back to me and Miles.

'Good thing I know a few lingos,' he said. 'I used to have Hans on the steam shovel but he ran out of puff. I picked him up for a couple of packets of fags, in Germany after the war. He was in the SS – Sausage Salvage. He used to collect the old sausage skins and fill them with sawdust for recycling. He was the recyclist champion and won the German Tour de France in 1940. He got a medal for it: the cast iron double cross with oak leaves and clusters.'

I noticed a bulge in one of the walls. I pointed it out to the foreman.

'Shh!' he whispered. 'We don't like to talk about it. It's the lump.'

Miles and I went down the road to an inn. There was a beefy-looking man there who seemed to be keeping well in with the customers. It was the inn-keeper. He knew Miles. Miles had done him once for giving too much froth on the beer. He slapped Miles heartily on the back and knocked him through the door.

'If it isn't my old weight measuring friend,' he yelled and gave Miles another hefty slap for good measure. Miles picked himself up and went over to the bar.

'I hate these hearty types,' he said, 'they get on my wick. They put my back up. Anyway, I'll have a pint, a pork pie, a bag of crisps – caviar flavour – a pickled onion and a cigar. I watch a lot of TV, you know.'

We sat down at a table. It turned out to be none other than my old friend Shortstuff. I apologised as he wiped the beer slops and a potato crisp from the top of his head.

Miles bought him eight shorts before he sobered down.

'Being short,' he said 'has always made life difficult for me. I was always getting the short end of the stick. I had a girl once. I thought it was the real thing at last. How well I remember! We cuddled in a hammock.'

'What happened?' I asked.

'We fell out,' he said.

Shortstuff knocked back another couple of shorts before going on. 'The trouble is,' he said, 'things never seem to go right for me. Like I had a toothache. I stuck it for a couple of years, but finally I had to go to my dentist – a real crab apple, known as Butcherboy Bragge. He loved me like pepper up his nostrils.

'"So!" said old Butcherboy, slapping me into the chair, "you've finally come to have it out with me. Ha-ha and tee-hee! What we call in the trade a rear extraction."

'I tell you, Tommy, it was murder. He nearly pulled off my head, and left my teeth. I said to him that I had been told he was a painless dentist. He lied in my teeth.

'"I am", he said. "It didn't hurt me one bit." And what is more, he ate garlic. I didn't need gas.

'Butcherboy Bragge got together with some other dentists and formed a group. They called themselves The Molars. They stuck to their gums and all their extractions were foreign. I hope all their teeth evaporate.

'People are always taking the mickey out of me, let alone using my head for a table top. They'll come up to me and say, "Could you use a few bob, Shortstuff? You look a bit short," and, "You look like you're in a rut, Shortstuff. That's what comes of drinking shorts."

'To tell the truth, I'm so fed up, I'm thinking of emigrating.'

'Where to?' I asked.

'To Central Africa' said Shortstuff, 'where the pigmies live. Where else?'

He suddenly rushed out and took a short cut to the back.

Soon after, a man walked over to our table. It was Bill Broome who had been a sweeper with a local football team. He had recently been commissioned by the Coalboard Navy to serve as a minesweeper.

'Why, hello, Tommy,' he said and tipped my beer into my lap. Into my lap! Just like that.

'Are you trying to say something?' I said, giving him one of my stern looks.

'Why, yes,' he said. 'I'm doing, "Who Do you Do?" I seek them here: I seek them there: I . . .'

'Wait!' I said. 'What has tipping beer into my lap got to do with it?'

'Well,' said Broome. 'I hear Harry is a big tipper. Yuk-yuk, yuk!'

'Yuk, yuk, yuk! is my bit,' I said.

I tipped a full ashtray over his head.

'I'm quite a big tipper, myself,' I said. 'That's a rubbish tip. Now take my tip and push off.'

'Ah!' sighed Miles. 'The world is full of nuts. Not like the old days. Everything has changed.'

'Profound! Profound!' I said. 'Now take these pies. Before the war they had pork in them.'

'No doubt the pork has dried up since then,' said Miles, 'it doesn't keep forever.'

'Cooking has changed,' I said. 'Now take plum duff or spotted dick. My mum used to make it in a good old woollen sock. It doesn't taste the same in a nylon sock, though I'll grant you can cook two at a time in a pair of tights.'

'You are right,' said Miles. 'Take saveloys. In the old days a hot dog was a hot dog.'

'Right!' I said. 'The hottest dog I've seen lately was sitting on the gas stove. It was a range rover.'

'Right!' said Miles, 'and if you go to any crummy restaurant nowadays, what do you get? What do you get? I ask you.'

75

'Right!' I said. 'I was in a restaurant the other day and asked for the cheeseboard. That's what I got. The cheeseboard without any cheese.'

'Right!' said Miles, 'you used to go into a restaurant and you would get boar's head, fillet steak and a brace of partridge. Then they would serve you the main course. And you would get change out of a ten shilling note, which is English for 50p.'

'Right!' I said, 'and what do you get now? Non starters at high prices. You need to take out a mortgage to take someone out to dinner, or sell your house.'

'Right!' said Miles, 'and in the old days if you couldn't pay your bill, you could work it off by doing the washing up.'

'Right!' I said, 'and now you would have to do the washing up for a year, and pay P.A.Y.E. and National Health, for one meal at the Saveloy Grill.'

'Right!' said Miles.

'Right?' I said. 'It's not right at all. It's all wrong. It's enough to make you lose your appetite. Have another pork pie before you cry.'

'No thanks,' said Miles. 'I'll just have a packet of crisps – pork pie flavour, another pint and a pickled onion.'

Miles looked around the room, very moody like. He was toying with his pickled onion and shaking his head sadly.

'It's a hard world,' he said. 'Everyone is having a tough time. D'you know, I've collected so many hard luck tales, I'm thinking of opening a shop retailing Manx cats. Things are getting worse all the time. I'm fed up to the teeth and even further. Everything is rotten. It's a dog's life. But who's complaining?'

At that moment a man breezed in singing, 'I've just come down from the Isle of Skye'.

'Why!' exclaimed the landlord. 'It's my old flying

instructor, the Reverend Angus McKay. He's a Skye pilot.'

Angus ordered another pint of beer and started conversation with one and all about his RAF days.

'I was in the RAF,' said Miles. 'I flew in Wellingtons.'

'I always wore flying boots myself,' said Angus.

Another chap was hovering around and he joined in the conversation. He had also been in the RAF it turned out.

'What are you doing now?' asked Angus.

'Just hovering around,' said the man, hovering around. 'I'm a craftman. I'm a hovercraftsman. I piloted hovercrafts during the election. The idea was to pick up floating voters.'

'What about you?' asked Angus, looking at me. 'Were you ever in the RAF?'

'Me? No,' I said, 'I was in the Horse Guards.'

'What did you have to guard them from?' asked Angus.

'From horse-flies,' I said. 'They're very clever are horse-flies. I once heard two of them talking:

"Y'know," said one fly, "human beings are real stupid. Real stupid. They spend lots of time and money building walls and ceilings then spend all their time walking on the floors".'

'Highly hilarious', said Angus.

He looked at his watch.

'My!' he exclaimed. 'Look at the time, how it flies! I've so much to do and I'm due at the airfield at midnight. I've got to fly.'

'He's just a fly-by-night,' said the landlord.

'Before I go,' Angus said, 'let us sing that stirring song dedicated to those brave men who fought in the skies in the Battle of Britain. To the glorious few.'

We all joined in singing, 'Few were the only Girl in the World'.

There was a sudden disturbance. It was the Mad Pole

from Polegate. He was waving a barber's pole and shouting, 'Pretty Pole! Pretty Pole! Who's a pretty boy, then?' He next hummed the overture to *The Barber of Seville*. Then he shaved the bearded lady from the circus, who happened to be in the bar at the time. It was a close shave. He had only just left when her husband Magnus the Mighty walked in. Magnus didn't recognise his wife straight away, but when he did, he was fighting mad. They began shouting and hurling insults and threats.

Miles ignored them. He was in an ignorant mood.

'I'll have another packet of crisps,' he said, 'and I think it would be nice if I could have potato flavour for a change. I wonder if there is such a thing?'

10

Lord Grousemore

I WAS STAYING for a few weeks, with my old friend Lord Grousemore at his stately home, up on the moors. He invited me to do a spot of grouse shooting. We shot anybody who groused (except Lord Grousemore, that is).

He told me all about game. He taught me all about pheasants, woodcocks, partridges and snipes. I came out one morning and shot a bird on the roof. It was a gutter snipe. The next day I bagged a brace of partridge in a peartree. It was a fine pair.

Lord Grousemore told me he often went to a fancy dress ball dressed as a partridge just to show how game he was. Once he had gone as a pheasant. Everyone had said it was a pheasant surprise.

We were out in the grounds one day. There was a sudden disturbance. It was the Mad Moor from Moorgate singing 'On Ilkley moor bah tat'. Lord Grousemore dropped his monocle and nearly jumped out of his knickerbockers. His double-barrelled shotgun went off. It disappeared down the path in a cloud of dust. It frightened a huge bull. It came charging at us. I took the bull by the horns and threw it. It was easy. I've thrown a lot of bull in my time.

'Bully for you, Cooper,' said Lord Grousemore. 'Let's go into the library for drinkies. Bull's blood from Hungary, to celebrate.'

His secretary was in the library. She was doing the book-keeping. She left as we walked in.

'She's a nice girl,' said his lordship, 'and I'm going to give her a mink coat.'

'I knew a burglar once,' I said, 'who gave his wife a mink coat. He told her it was worth at least five years.'

The old boy put his monocle on his ear and told me to speak up.

'I like you, Cooper,' he said. 'You've got such an open face. You should try and shut it more often. However, I will say this. You don't get up to any tricks.'

I wasn't sure how to take that. After all, I'm a magician, not just an open face. I felt I had to prove myself.

'Lord Grousemore,' I said, 'I'll perform a feat of magic for you. Why! I'll saw a lady in half. That is if we had a lady.'

'Capital!' said the old boy, 'I'll ring for my secretary. I'm sure she's never been sawn in half.'

I changed the subject.

Lord Grousemore liked to brag about his ancestors.

'Y'know, Tommy?' he said to me, 'one of my ancestors was the executioner at the time of the French Revolution. He was a whiz at the old guillotine dodge. It was difficult for a fellow to keep his head. My ancestor was kept so busy, he complained that he was running out of baskets. He had to keep all his heads in one basket. He was a proper head-case.'

I chuckled to myself and to Lord Grousemore's self. I was feeling a little selfish.

'I want my tea,' decided Lord Grousemore then, 'I'll ring for the butler.' He picked up the telephone and dialled International Telephones.

'He's from Australia,' he explained.

The butler came in. He looked guilty.

'Been peeping through the keyholes again?' said the old boy. 'What did you see this time?'

I was interested in what the butler had seen but Lord

Grousemore waved his monocle at the end of its rope.

'Never mind,' he said irritably. 'I want my tea, Sneed.'

He called the butler Sneed because that was his name and he didn't like it.

'Very good m'lord,' said Sneed, tucking his ruffled starched shirt back in his boots. 'Will that be all, Sir?'

'No, Sneed,' said the old boy, 'I'll have a boiled egg. Make sure it's a hen's egg.'

He gave his monocle a couple of dangles and wedged it in his left nostril.

'Yes,' said Lord Grousemore, 'one has to be careful, what with all these imported eggs nowadays. D'you know, Tommy, crocodiles lay eggs? Sneed brought me one for breakfast by mistake. Leastwise that's what he said. Anyway, I broke it open and it bit the spoon off. Mind you, it didn't taste all that bad, though it was hard to pick out the teeth. One has to be careful with one's food all the same.'

'You're so right, your serene majesty' I said.

'We're friends,' protested the old boy, 'just call me "Your highness," Cooper.'

'Well,' I humbled, 'as I was saying. I was at a card party once. We were served steak sandwiches and game pie. The steaks were high and so was the game. I felt sick, I threw up the game.'

'I see what you mean,' said the old boy. 'You're quite a card yourself, Cooper. You must show me some more card tricks.'

He handed me a box of assorted rissoles.

'Try one of these,' he said, 'the soft centres are delicious. They're all handmade.'

He was right. I found a glove in mine to prove it.

'I'll show you a card trick,' I said. 'It's taken me years to perfect and I've still not perfected it.'

I produced a deck of cards out of thin air.

'Now,' I said, 'pick a card out of the pack. Any card!'

'Yes,' said the old boy. 'I'll take this card. It is the deuce of diamonds.'

'Right!' I said. 'Right, first time!'

'Remarkable,' said his lordship. 'How the deuce do you do it? You must show me that some time, Cooper. I'm sure I'll baffle my friends at the club with that trick. Ah! But what if I had selected the ace of clubs? But no matter.'

He offered me another rissole.

'Y'know, Cooper,' he said, 'I saw you once on the wireless. I thought you were familiar.'

'You mean on TV,' I said.

'Was it?' said the old boy. 'You do surprise me. We don't have TV. But, then, we are living in a wonderful age.'

I heard a ringing in my ears. It was my ear-rings. The butler came in.

'You rang m'lord?' he asked.

'No,' said his lordship. 'I won't ring you: you ring me. Don't confuse the issue. Goodbye and good luck and remember to blow out the lights on the gas-stove.'

Lord Grousemore scratched his nose with his monocle.

'He's getting old,' he said. 'You don't get retainers like that nowadays.'

'I'm sure you're right,' I said. 'Everyone has an angle.'

'Do you like angling?' asked his lordship. 'We've got salmon here, y'know.'

'Ah!' I said. 'We often had poached salmon at home. My uncle was a poacher.'

'Interesting,' said the old boy. 'On this estate we've got hare and rabbit. I could get Sneed to poach you a rabbit for breakfast.'

Lord Grousemore glanced at his monocle and shook it.

'It's getting late,' he said. 'Do another trick, Cooper.'

I did one of my rope tricks.

'That was a bit ropey,' he said.

'I can do a marvellous trick with twenty balls of string,' I said.

82

'Hmm!' he said. 'That certainly sounds like a lot of
. . . uh . . . string to me.'

'I'll tell you what,' I said. 'I'll recite for you instead.
It's a little poem I wrote when I was in Finland:

I once saw a comic called Pinky,
Do a one man show in Helsinki;
I thought, for my money,
That he was quite funny,
But the critics said he was stinky.

'Ah,' said Lord Grousemore. 'Was he Finnish?'

'No,' I said, 'he was fattish.'

At that moment, the butler came in with two big dogs.

'I'm taking the beagles for walkies,' he said.

'Very good,' exclaimed Lord Grousemore. 'But be
back in time to help me do the teas.'

He turned to me and scratched his monocle.

'I show people around the old stately home,' he said,
'and old Sneed helps me dish out the teas at 10p a slop.'

'Do you like beagles?' he asked.

'Not black beagles,' I said. 'I like salmon beagles or
ones with cream cheese.'

The cook came in wringing her hands.

'Stop that wringing,' said his lordship. 'You'll have
Sneed running in. What is it?'

'I just put a dozen chickens in the freezer,' she said.
'You should've heard them screech.'

'Chicken out!' said Lord Grousemore dismissing her
with a wave of his monocle.

'Do you like domestic animals, Cooper? I do passable
farm-yard imitations, myself.'

He yodelled, flapped his arms and flew round the room
a couple of times.

'Come on, Cooper,' he said. 'I'll show you around my
farm.'

We put on our wellies and sheepskin coats and went off. The first thing I saw was a couple of pigs blocking our path.

'Ho!' said the old boy, 'the swine are hogging the road.'

'They're just a couple of old boars,' muttered an old sow. She went off snorting, 'There was a farmer, had an old sow . . .'

She dropped something. I picked it up. It was a ballpoint, a pig pen.

'See a pen and pick it up and all the day you'll have good luck . . .' said his lordship.

I stepped into something ankle-deep outside the cowshed.

'How lucky can you get?' remarked the old boy.

We went into the cowshed. I was smellbound. The cows were being milked by electric milking machines. One cow was being milked by a milking machine for the first time.

'How do you like that?' asked his lordship.

Before I could reply, the cow gave a moo-moo and said: 'It's udder this world. It's udderly marvellous. It's far superior to the udder way.'

We left her squirting away happily.

Next, we watched a sheepdog at work. It was driving a flock of sheep. I saw it make a ewe turn and ram a ram. It looked rather sheepish.

After that we went to visit his lordship's poultry farm. He introduced me to his manager. His name was Sam Pecker. He looked henpecked. He certainly was broody. He was

an egghead and we caught him with egg on his face. He
had a cockscomb and was wearing a feathered shirt with
a chicken wing collar, jodphurs, bobby sox and dancing
pumps. He had on a porkpie hat. Real porkpie. He
clucked when he talked. He explained to me all about
poultry: how you can tell a Rhode Island Red by its left
wing, an Aylesbury duckling because it comes from
Aylesbury and a Norfolk Turkey because it comes from
Turkey.

While we were there, the hens were working like
balmy. They were laying eggs on the conveyor belt and
going back for more.

There was a sudden disturbance. It was the Mad Cock
from Cockermouth singing, 'Cockadoodle-doo'.

'Ah,' said Sam. 'It's time for their elevenses. Would
you care to join us?'

'No, thanks,' I said, 'that's chicken feed to me. I'll join
Lord Grousemore for cocktails. To tell the truth, I only
care for chicken, fried, roasted or in sandwiches or . . .'

Sam went pale.

'Shh!' he whispered. 'Don't speak like that in front of
the chickens.'

'Try crossing chicken with your pigs,' I said to his
lordship. 'The hens will lay eggs and bacon.'

'We tried it,' said the old boy. 'The eggs came out
streaky. Now stop egging Sam on. We had better leave
him to get on with it. He's got the afternoon off. He's
going to visit his grandmother. She lives at Egham. He's
teaching her to suck eggs.'

Lord Grousemore sucked his monocle dreamily.

'So long, Sam,' he said. 'Keep your pecker up.'

'Up what?' muttered Sam. He crowed, and laid an egg.

We went back to the house for cocktails. I said to Lord
Grousemore: 'There's a big crack down the side of your
cocktail cabinet.'

'It's just a cabinet split,' he replied. 'Which reminds

85

me,' he continued, 'have you ever met my nephew, the dishonourable Phillip Phelps, spelt with two effs? He's a super salesman y'know. He lobbied his MP and sold him a government whip. He had heard that a new foreign secretary had been appointed and wanted to know why the job hadn't been given to an Englishman. He would have made a good politician himself. He's the chairman of the local swimming club.'

Lord Grousemore dangled his monocle in his cocktail and dried it on his necktie.

'Y'know, Cooper,' he said. 'If you really want to be in the swim, you must join our swimming club. You will have to go before a selection committee. It's a diving board.'

So I went before the board and was asked a lot of questions. Soon my head was swimming. The chairman kept going off the deep end.

'Look, Cooper,' he said, 'you will have to pass certain tests before you are permitted to join our club. Come out to our swimming baths.'

'Yes, Cooper,' said the vice-chairman, 'do as the chairman asks.'

I went to the pool and did twenty lengths. Then the chairman yelled: 'Get out of the paddling pool, and let's see you perform.'

'Let's see you perform,' echoed the vice-chairman.

I jumped into the water. I climbed out to change into bathing shorts.

'Let's see you crawl,' said the chairman.

I went towards him on my hands and knees.

'That's not quite right,' said the chairman.

'Not right at all. Our chairman is right,' said the vice-chairman, 'you'll have to do better than that if you want to make a splash here.'

'Well, let's see *you* crawl,' I said to the vice-chairman. 'Seems to me, you're the biggest crawler around here.'

I ducked out and went off through the village back to Lord Grousemore's mansion. On the way I passed the old mill. I could hear the old miller singing, 'There's a wholemeal by the stream'.

Next to the mill, builders were working on the roof of a house. Half the thatching had already been replaced with tiles. It was a semi-dethatched cottage.

I was reminded of a Christmas I had spent with Lord Grousemore. I gave a show in the local branch of the British Legion. There was a Christmas tree and the holly hung round the walls. We, naturally, sang 'It was Christmas day in the workhouse', and I did sum tricks. Two plus two is four. Three threes are nine, and similar ones. The audience multiplied, but they were divided in their reaction. I was told to get cubed when none of it added up. The metric jokes didn't go down too well either! I heard their feet inching towards the door. By then I was miles away. I never looked back.

11

Whose Zoo?

I LOVE ANIMALS. I love going to zoos, menageries and safari packs. That's why I bought myself a safari suit. There are lots of zoos all over the country. Some are owned by Earls and Lords and suchlike. You'll find them all in *Whose Zoo?*

I like the way the camels bow to me when they see me in my fez. Camels are like elephants, they never forget. I once met a camel in the London Zoo. We had last met in Egypt during the war. I recognised him by his sneer. He saw me and curled his lip. He knew me right away. He tried to bite me. I was the one who had given him the hump. As a matter of fact, I was wearing a camel coat at the time. It still had the hump on the back.

I went to Whipsnade Zoo. What a day! As I went in, I could hear Shirley Temple singing 'Animal Crackers'.

I saw some animals playing poker. One had five aces. It was a cheetah. Another player was very strange to look at. I recognised it was a yak when it started to laugh at the jackass. It went, 'Yah, yak-yak!' Just like that.

Most of the monkeys were going about their business, carrying out their inspections and sorting each other out. One group of monkeys was having a tea party. It was none other than the monkeys of the TV tea commercials. They were having a fine old time. They were really lapping it up. One poured tea over the head of another and said: 'Ah! The tea you can really waste.'

'What tea is it then, Syd?' the monkey asked. 'It doesn't taste too good.'

'I'm not surprised, Alf,' said Syd. 'It is VAT.'

'Tastes more like CAT if you ask me' said Alf. 'Where's the sugar, then?'

One monkey, they called him Monkey Bob, said, 'I used it all for *my* TUC.'

There was Rosie, the red-faced monkey, and Booboo the blue-armed baboon. They kept picking on each other. It was quite a party.

I saw a keeper trying to get a tiger back into its cage. He had the tiger by the tail. A singing quartet of keepers were singing 'Hold that Tiger'. The tiger was baying like a dog. It was from Tiger Bay.

The wolves were eyeing passing girls and giving wolf whistles. One was wearing a sheepskin coat.

I overheard three kids who were admiring a huge bird in a cage. The conversation was rapid and went something like this:

'Sneagle!'

'Snot. Snawk!'

'Sneither. Snostritch!'

Actually it was a big buzzard. It was smoking a pipe. It was a condor.

I saw a hyena. I told it a joke. It stopped laughing. I watched leopards changing their spots. They moved from one spot to another. One moved to a guest spot. I saw some striped leopards and spotted zebras. The leopards had played football with the zebras and after the match they changed jerseys. I saw a bison. It was a pudding-bison.

90

I struck up a conversation with a Chinese girl in the snake house.

'You're a real charmer,' I said.

'That's a lot of cobras,' she said.

One snake was counting the snakes climbing ladders. It was an adder. He was wheeling the pram with a kid in it. It was shaking a snake. It was a rattlesnake. The kid's father was an old goat. He kept trying to butt in.

There was a sudden disturbance. It was the Mad Boar from Boreham Wood. He was boring holes in the road and singing 'The High Top Hat my Feather Boa, fifty years ago'. It upset an old deer who was trying to break into a stag party.

I saw a polar bear. It was trying to balance on a glacier mint. A monkey was filling a jaguar with petrol. I stood by the kerb and watched a pelican crossing. A couple of giraffes were necking in broad daylight. They had a lot of neck. The boxing kangaroo was challenging all comers. He met his match in the Kung Fu Kangaroo. It nearly kicked the stuffing out of him.

The elephants were packing their trunks for the weekend. An old bull elephant was in charge. He kept prodding them with his tusks. He was a hard tusk-master.

I poodled along to the book kiosk for some books on animals. It was chock-full with penguins, corgis and pelicans. They were crowding the shelves so I went back to my car.

I found a snake on the windscreen. It was a windscreen viper. On the verge I saw a snake in the grass. It was a traffic warden. She was chatty. She told me she came from a long line of wardens. Her grandfather had been a prison warden, her father an air-raid warden and her uncle a church warden. Personally, I thought she might be a game warden but I was in a hurry to get home.

12

Take it in your Stride

WHEN OLD SYD DIED, he was barely one hundred and
five. He had been a cricketer all his life, but this
was the highest score he had ever knocked up. He
dropped dead over a wicket gate and the coroner brought
in a verdict of lbw.

We all reckoned that old Syd had had a good innings
and we went to see him off. It was the last day of the Tests
in Australia.

His old partner, George, arrived from Afghanistan with
his wife, cycling all the way on a tandem. They left it
double-parked outside the roof-restaurant of the Post
Office Tower. The wife looked like King Kong in drag.
To tell the truth, I kept well out of her way. I think she
thought I fancied her.

George's eyes were mournful. His nose hung down
like an old saveloy and his chins drooped over his
collar. He was wearing a horse collar. He was also
wearing an armpit-length duffle-coat trimmed with lace.
Smoke was coming out of his hat. It was a stove-pipe
hat. He raised the brim to the ladies. The crown
remained on his head. He was smoking a double-
barrelled cigar in a gas-pipe.

The last rites and wrongs were conducted by Mad Vic,
the vicar from Vicarstown.

When he came to the 'ashes to ashes . . .' part George
turned to me. 'Talking about ashes,' he said, 'do you
know the latest Test scores?'

'No,' I said, 'ask old Syd. He's down under.'

At that moment the pall bearers appeared bearing their palls: a cat crept into a crypt and crept out again; and a Polish athlete was laid to rest in a vault. It was a pole vault.

There was a sudden disturbance. It was the Mad Grave-digger from Gravesend. He was trying to get on the gravy train. He said it was really his day off, but he had been asked to fill in for a friend.

'All right,' said the vicar, 'dig in.'

The sexton appeared with a skull in his hand. He started to recite, 'To bier, or not to bier. That is the question.'

Soon after the funeral, I went to Oxford where I appeared at the New Theatre. On the same bill was Signor Stradivarius, the veteran violinist. He was an old fiddler. He played, 'Tales from Hoffman' and 'Tales from Hoffwoman'.

I stayed in a boarding house that catered for students and graduates. We had college pudding every day. One of the graduates had very short well-trimmed hair and a goatee beard. Her name was Nanette. She was called Nanny for short. When she walked down the street in her cap and gown, everyone stared at her. It was her nightcap and nightgown.

I got talking to her one night in the kitchen. She was fixing herself a snack – a sago sandwich and a cup of senna tea. She told me that her mother was in show business.

'She's a stripper,' she said, 'and if that isn't show

business, I don't know what is. She shows just about everything. Sometimes I get the urge to be a streaker myself. It must be something in the blood. Have you ever seen a streaker, Tommy?'

'Well,' I said, 'I knew a man who did a streak once, but he was fully clothed. He streaked through a nudist colony. I also know a duck who is a streaker.'

After the Spring season at Oxford in 1972, I recorded some shows for Thames Television. All the family were thrilled.

And talking of my family, when I first got married my in-laws said they were going to show me their joint savings. They took me to a huge safe. It was full of joints. He was a butcher. I used to get out of his way pretty sharpish if I ever saw him girding his loins. He once took a lump of steak and threw it at me. It was chuck steak. He wanted to use my head to chop meat. He said it was a mental block. He used sticks to chop chops. They were chop sticks. While he worked he used to sing 'Butcher arms around me'. If you asked him 'How's business' he used to reply 'Offal'.

Anyway, one day at the recording studio, an electrician came to see me in my dressing room.

'Mr Cooper', he said, 'someone has nicked me strides.'

'Your what?' I said.

'Nicked me strides, me round-the-houses – me trousers,' he said.

'But . . .,' I began.

'But nothing,' he said. 'Them strides are mighty important to me. They're special. I only just had them made into parallels. They've been altered from twenty-four inch bottoms to eighteens. They've been narrowed to drainpipes. I've worn 'em as pegtops and they've been flared twice. That was some job, flaring them, I can tell you. I had to use the material from me weskit. I've worn 'em with turn-ups and without turn-ups. When I first had them they were blue, then I dyed 'em green, then I dyed 'em pink to match me shirt which I had tapered. I've had the waistband let out four times and a vee cut in the back. I know me strides inside out. There's a hole in the left hand side pocket. An' one day a man in the tube was standing with his foot in me pocket and he had sharp toe nails. I lost a 2p through the hole he made.'

'Look,' I said.

'You, look,' he interrupted, 'what do you think I look like coming to work in my underpants like this? Wait! I'll tell you. I look a proper sight, that's what. And people give me some funny looks travelling on the tube, I can tell you. Besides, I'm used to being dressed right fashionable.'

'You don't look too bad in your underpants,' I said, 'except one leg is longer than the other and you've got them inside out and back to front.'

'Don't be funny, Mr Cooper,' he said. 'This is very serious. Here's some man going around, showing off in me trousers and me walking about in me shorts.'

'OK' I said, 'you've made your point. But what's all this got to do with me? What can I do?'

'I'll tell you what you can do, Mr Cooper,' he said, 'you can take off me trousers that's what you can do. To tell the truth they're not your scene. They don't suit you at all. Give me back me strides.'

'I just borrowed them to paint the hall,' I said.

'Use a paint brush like other people,' he said, 'and give me back me strides.'

Well. You can't argue with some people. I felt the draught all the way back home that night.

13

A Dog's Life

THERE I WAS at the weather office, I wanted a weather report on road conditions. I was thinking of doing another road show. Portland Bill was in the office talking to Ronald Sway. They had just had a German Bight for lunch and were off to the Dogger Bank to cash their pay checks.

They told me to expect cold showers and warm spells and to be on the lookout for black ice, hot ice and cream ice. Ronald said the weather would be moist with heavy outbreaks of foot and mouth, but would brighten up between dawn and morning with a heavy ground swell. Bill advised me to take my sunglasses or my wellies and a barometer.

'File that report,' he said and gave Ronald a nail file.

Ronald filed a nail on the wall. I went out into the street into a blizzard. It was also snowing hard. So I popped across the street to see a friend of mine. He's a comedian. He had a gag writer with him. I knew he was a gagwriter. He was writing with a gag in his mouth and gagging on his own jokes.

'Hello, hello, hello!' my friend greeted me. 'Who was that lady I saw you with last night?' he said.

'My wife,' I said. 'What else is new?'

'I've just been made a director of our football club,' he said.

'The only director they need,' I said, 'is a funeral director'.

'Charming!' he said. 'There are worse teams.'

'Well,' I replied, 'I once went to a football match in South America, it was a rough game. The kickoff was a real kickoff. Five men were kicked off, including the referee. He went to wet his whistle. As he was leaving the field someone shouted "Shoot". There was a volley of shots and he had to run for his life. After the game, both teams were suspended. By their necks. One of the home team was a man who was a professional announcer. Whenever he was tackled he talked his way out of it. He was always on the ball. Yes. It was a very hairy game.'

'A hair-raising story, to be sure,' said my friend. 'I only half-heard it. I'm half-asleep. My quack told me to take half a sleeping pill. I took the prescription to the local chemist, Mr Geiger. He was standing at his counter. He was lobbing out radioactive supports for atomic fallouts, ointment for guestspots, penicillin for National Health patients and tenpenicillin for private patients, and capsules for astronauts. There were also senna pods and tripods for sluggish three-legged racers – that was on the Grand National Health.

'I met Dicky Bird there. As you know he's a bird fancier. His special fancy is pigeons. He, himself, is pigeon-toed and pigeon-chested. Anyway, that's his pigeon. He told me he was getting something for one of his pigeons. It was suffering from chicken spots. As a matter of fact, what Dicky doesn't know about pigeons could be covered by a pigeon spot. And the pigeons know him. They can spot him from a mile off, and they often do. He is known as Spotted Dick. He has a dog, a black labrador. Everyone thinks it is a dalmation. One of Dick's pigeons likes to fly over trains. It is a train spotter. Another flies over football matches. It likes spotting the ball.

'I once met one of Dick's pigeons in Italy. It had just

spotted a policeman. It had caught his eye and what the policeman was saying didn't sound at all nice. He caught the pigeon and jammed it in a pigeon hole. At that moment there was a sudden disturbance. It was the Mad Vatman from the Vatican singing, "Vat d'you want if you don't vant money?" He had more faith than Adam.'

'Oh yes,' continued my friend, 'Dicky is a queer bird, to be sure. He came home one evening from bird-song. He caught his wife with the man from the Prudential. He was aghast. "Now I know everything," he cried.

'"Good", said his wife. "So why don't you go in for the Bird-Brain of Britain contest? Why don't you?" Not that she is so smart. I heard her remark one day that she never found marrow bones in any marrow she bought. I explained to her that a marrow just misses being a cucumber by a marrow margin and you can't pick any bones out of that.'

I gave him the bird. I went off in the direction of Wardour Street wrapped in thought and a heavy overcoat. I suddenly got the horrible feeling that one of my legs was shorter than the other. I remember the way my mother was always pulling my leg. I looked down and saw I was walking with one foot in the gutter. I gave a sigh of relief and continued with both feet in the gutter.

There was a sudden disturbance. It was Mad Stan from Stanmore shouting, 'Stan and deliver!' I stood on his foot and delivered a right-hander. He was hopping mad. He hopped off in the direction of Pimlico shouting, 'Stan aside! Stan back!' shaking his head, a leg and a fist. I ran into him again a few days later. Unfortunately for him I was in my car at the time.

I went into a pub. Two men I know were there at the bar. One was Sam Houston, the Texas oil baron. The other was Sir Ali Baba, the Arabian Knight.

'Well, well, well!' said the Texan.

'Well, well, well, well, well,' said Sir Ali, 'and I could go on all night.'

The Texan got his rag out. It was an oil rag. They were still well-welling when I left. I got home late and my wife was mad at me.

'One day,' she threatened, 'I'm going to catch you out.'

Well, I was back in the bar a few days later, sitting quietly in a corner chatting about this, that and the other. I was completely on my own. Not another soul in the place. Suddenly my wife walked in.

'Barman! Barman!' she yelled. 'Where are you?'

The barman appeared, grumbling and adjusting his tie.

'Yes, madame?' he enquired.

'I'll have the same as him,' my wife said pointing in my direction.

He poured her a stiff drink. She knocked it back. She clutched the back of her head, coughing and spluttering.

'Muddy hell!' she choked, 'how can you drink that muddy awful stuff?'

'See!' I said, 'now you know. And all the time you thought I was enjoying myself.'

I took her to a posh restaurant. A couple with a youngster were just leaving. The woman turned to the waiter.

'I say my good fellow,' she said, very snooty and old fashioned like. 'I would like some scraps to take home for the dog. Have you a doggy bag?'

'Wow!' yelled the little boy. 'Are you really going to get a dog?'

The woman was foxed. The boy doggedly repeated the

question. My wife hounded me out of the restaurant. It was one of those nights.

14

Cooper the Snooper

SOME YEARS AGO I was in New York. I was invited to a Police Precinct Station downtown, there I met Kojak. Columbo was there too, on an exchange visit from Los Angeles.

Now, I've had a good deal of experience on the old detective dodge myself. I've watched Z Cars, Softly Softly and The Sweeney, so I know what I'm talking about. I offered to join forces with Columbo and Kojak. I suggested we call ourselves The Three Cs. Cooper, Kojak and Columbo. A deadly combination.

I needed a gimmick like Kojak's lollipops, and Columbo's mac. Well, I had my fez and I put it on. A passing detective asked me if I knew someone had dropped a flowerpot on my head.

It was nearing lunchtime. I popped across to the grill-room. Kojak was grilling a suspect known as Dum-Dum. He had a bullet head. Soon the guy was singing like a canary. He sang, 'There's a song they sing at a sing-song in Sing Sing'.

'What d'you know?' said Kojak, 'this baby will sing, but he won't talk.'

Columbo came in and lit a cigar. He stuck the lighted end in his mouth.

'Call me hot lips,' he spluttered, 'I've just had a real hot tip.'

He smacked himself on the head. He knocked himself cold. Kojak started giving him the kiss of life.

The Chief walked in.

'Watch it Kojak,' he said, 'you know how one thing can lead to another.'

Columbo woke up.

'Ah! Lemme see,' he said to Kojak. 'You've been eating garlic.'

'Y'know,' said Kojak, 'I'm going to let my hair down and tell you something; you're quite a detective. But we'll have a few facts. I've not been eating garlic at all; just hamburgers and raw onions. I don't want you to get the wrong impression'.

Columbo was about to slap himself on the head again, but thought better of it. He slapped Kojak instead. Kojak didn't turn a hair.

The three of us went out to the street together. It was raining. Columbo took off his mac. It was the first time I had seen him without it. I didn't recognise him at first.

Kojak made a sudden dive across the road to where there was a pedestrian crossing. He threw him to the ground. It was a lollipop man. Kojak said: 'I'm looking for you,' and then popped the man's head in his mouth.

I decided it was time for me to make a move. I scratched my fez and stopped a suspicious looking person wearing diamond ear-rings. He was wheeling a pram. He was a pusher.

'Y'know,' said Kojak, 'some pussycat whispered in my ear that none other than Hotfoot Harry is holed up in a hole in the wall in Hester Street. He totes a double-barrelled shotgun in his pants pocket, so don't upset him. He is such a character as is liable to go off at half cock, at the drop of a hat. So don't go dropping any hats when he's around, y'know?'

We went into this fleabag down on the lower East Side and broke into Hotfoot Harry's room. He wasn't around. I went to raise the blind. It was just a blind. Behind it was just a blank wall.

'Search the joint,' said Kojak. 'We might find the gun.'

He looked under the bed. It wasn't there. We eventually found it in the closet.

'Well, I guess that is all,' said Kojak.

I thought that was a bald statement coming from him and I said as much.

Kojak gave me one of his curly looks.

'Cooper-schmooper!' he said, 'what are you? Some sort of a nut? Anyone can see you haven't got a clue on this caper. It's obvious that Hotfoot Harry has hotfooted it right out of this joint.'

'Wait!' I said, 'we haven't had a look in the study.'

Columbo smacked himself on the forehead and his cigar popped out of his mouth.

Kojak pushed open the door, and there was Hotfoot Harry studying a paper. It was a racing paper. It raced out of the room. We had caught him.

'What's the matter, fellas,' he whined, 'can't a guy have any privacy nowadays?'

'Dog it!' said Kojak, 'and brace yourself. I'm slapping the old arm on you.'

He did and nearly knocked Hotfoot through the floor.

'You had no call to do that,' said Hotfoot. 'Harry O wouldn't do a thing like that nor, for that matter, would old Ironside, and as everyone knows, he's a very hard case, to be sure.'

Kojak ignored him and turned to me.

'Go call a cop, Cooper,' he said. 'We'll hand him over. We've got other fish to fry. There's something fishy going on in the Fulton Fish Market. We're going there on a fishing expedition.'

In the car on the way across town, Kojak told us what it was all about.

'We're going after a guy called Fishball Finnigan,' he said. 'He's trying to muscle in on the oyster smuggling racket. He's a real weirdo. He smoked salmon and lobster pot and wears fishnet stockings. He always hangs out where the big fish are.'

'I remember seeing him once in Frisco, down on Fisherman's Wharf,' said Columbo. 'He was with Fishcake Flannigan, the Kingfish of the waterfront. He had fish fingers in every fish pie – and that's official.'

He slapped his head suddenly. His ear fell off.

'We must be there,' he said. 'I smell fish.'

'Y' know,' said Kojak, 'you're quite a detective. As a matter of fact you are quite right about the fish. What you can smell is a fishcake sandwich. It's been in my pocket since last Saturday. Thanks for reminding me about it.'

He took out the sandwich and gave us all a bite.

'May I make a suggestion?' said Columbo. 'Why don't we disguise ourselves? I will wear your hat, Kojak, and you will wear Cooper's.'

'What will I wear?' I asked.

'You can wear a new hairstyle,' said Columbo. 'We'll stop off at Jake the Barbers and get your head shaved. Kojak can get his head polished and have a blow-wave at the same time.'

'I'm not wearing that,' I said.

'Forget it,' said Kojak, 'Cooper's hat would spoil my image.'

We got off at the Fulton Fish Market and followed Kojak into a large warehouse on the waterfront. A man came up to us. He was a queer fish.

'I'm Mr Fishberg,' he said. 'I'm the manager here, can I help you?'

'You can and you will,' said Kojak, real friendly, 'or I'll bust your gut. What sort of place have you got here?'

'Well,' said Fishberg, very apologetic, 'we do not have much in the way of plaice just at present, but we've got some very fine fresh haddock, to be sure.'

Columbo picked up a haddock and examined it. Suddenly he slapped himself on the head. He was still holding the haddock and it wrapped itself round his face.

'I've just thought of something,' he said spluttering and spitting out fish scales. 'Outside, I saw a shark standing up against a capstan. It could have been Fishball in disguise. He was all on his lonesome.'

'That was just a loan shark,' said Kojak. 'Try borrowing a fin from it.'

We went outside to the quay. I was the first to spot Fishball. He was wearing a herringbone suit with real herringbones. He saw us and started to go for his gun. It was on a crate at the other end of the quay. He slipped on a skate. It was a roller skate. He rolled right up to us. He picked up a bar. It was a fishbar. Kojak ducked and hit him with a mop. It was a roll mop. Then Kojak slapped him around with a halibut.

'All right, all right, already!' yelled Fishball. 'Enough is enough. I ain't that crazy for halibut. I can see you're a keen angler. So tell me. What's your angle?'

'Button your lip, baby,' said Kojak. 'We've caught our fish. You've had your chips, Fishball.'

Kojak turned to me.

'Open that case, Cooper,' he said. 'There's the proof that he's been muscling in here.'

109

I opened the case. It was full of mussels.

'That's the clincher,' said Kojak. 'Grab a handful, Cooper, for evidence. Keep it under your hat.'

'Right!' I said, 'and now I've even got mussels on my brain.'

'By the way,' I said to Kojak, 'what do they do with all this mouldy fish here?'

'Why, what d'you think dummy?' said Kojak, 'they use it to make fish fungus.'

As we came alongside the wharf, I saw someone come round the corner, driving a tank. It was a fish tank.

There was a sudden disturbance. It was the Mad Fisherman from Fishguard. He was singing a sad ditty, 'If your lips cod only speak'. Kojak threw a squid at him. He shut up like a clam.

Kojak took a lollipop from behind his ear and popped it into his mouth.

'That wraps it up, baby,' he said. 'We've got a case as tight as a fish's ear which, as is known to one and all, is watertight.'

At that moment, there was a loud boom. We looked round.

'I thought as much,' said Columbo. 'See that guy over there sitting on two packing cases? That's Cannon, the well-known private eye from Frisco.'

'Sounds like he was was just fired,' said Kojak.

'Ah,' I said, 'then we can invite him to join us. We'll be the four Cs. Cooper, Kojak, Columbo and Cannon. How's that then?'

They looked at each other. It was all quiet on the waterfront. Something was wrong. They looked at each other again. The quiet on the waterfront was wearing a bit thin by now. That's it, I thought, no one has a clue! I went in search of one . . .

15

Sheikh of Araby

RECENTLY I WENT on a novel holiday with a man called Mad Mick. He was called Mad Mick because he was as cracked as a plate and as wild as oats. The idea was to trek across the Arabian desert in a Land Rover. Before I left everyone said I ought to get my head examined. So I went to the doctor to have my brains tested. The doctor couldn't find anything.

Now I'm no novice on the old desert dodge, but there we were one night, lost in the middle of the desert. Suddenly we heard drums. They were oil drums. Mad Mick, who had been with me in the Boy Scouts, had got his badge for fieldcraft, but as I pointed out it didn't include deserts.

'Don't fret, Tommy my old scout,' he said, 'I smell oil. There's an oilfield near here. Listen to those drums. This calls for oil-fieldcraft. Let's go!'

'Oil string along with you,' I said.

'I'm oil you got,' said Mad Mick.

Dawn came up. She had been out all night. We asked her where we could find the oilfield.

'It's over the second sand dune on the left just past the sandpits. I told the Sandman you were on the way,' she said. 'I'm off for a bathe in the sea. This is a long beach.'

'Yes,' I said, 'the tide's out. It'll take you two weeks to get down to the water.'

We went on and reached the oilfield. There was a large encampment and we soon found ourselves up to our shoulders in oil sheikhs.

We were escorted to a large tent. An important sheikh appeared. He was wrapped in a big robe. It had 'Claridges' woven right across the back.

'You're just in time for breakfast,' he said. 'I hope you like it. We're having my favourite, Champagne and pasties. Rolls Corniche pasties, of course.'

After breakfast the sheikh showed us around the place.

'See those men on the barrack square,' he said, 'they're drilling. And the band is the oil-pipe band of the Jordan Highlanders.'

They were wearing traditional hip-length kilts with ankle-length sporrans, and Glengarrys on their heads. They were being led by the Mad Camel of Camelford and were playing 'The Camels are Coming'.

That night the sheikhs held a party in our honour. It took seven of them to hold him. He was a big party. He was elected to be spokesman. The election was rigged. It was an oil rig.

We sat on cushions on the floor to eat.

I sat opposite a girl. She was making sheeps' eyes. I didn't like the look of them, but they were tasty. I made a ricket. I asked her to remove her yashmak. It wasn't a yashmak. It was just her beard.

'Now,' said the spokesman, 'we will have some entertainment. First you will see our lovely belly dancers dancing the new ballet, *The Oil-lake Ballet*. You will see our most beautiful ballerina, a genuine Arabesque. She will dance the dance of the seven veils. She will also do the Gaza Strip.'

There were lots of sheikhs present. Some had just come back from Mecca. They had gone to see the Miss World Contest.

Suddenly the spokesman shouted: 'Sheikh a leg, everybody' and everybody started dancing. Two sheikhs did the tango. It was the last tango. They danced sheikh to sheikh. Someone tapped me on the shoulder and asked me to dance. It was Marlon Brando. I said, 'No, but I admire your sheikh.'

I spotted a couple hanky-pankying under a coffee-table. They were sheikhing hands. We had community singing. We sang 'Sheikh, rattle and roll', and 'Roll out the oil-barrel'.

There was a sudden disturbance. It was Mad Jed from Jeddah. He wanted to know if anybody wanted some Jeddah cheese and biscuits.

The next morning we were invited to play a few rounds of Arabian Gulf. It was very difficult. All the holes kept filling up with oil. Our caddy was one of the dancers. He was called Mustapha, but he didn't say Mustapha what. He was known as the Nureyev of Arabia. He always carried a snack tucked in his loincloth.

There was an old lady peeping at us from between two hummocks of sand. It was a sand witch. Mustapha tucked her in his loincloth for later.

We ran into Sir Ali Baba again, the Arabian Knight. He was riding out of a sandcastle. Two little boys stood by with their buckets and spades.

'Hello!' he said, 'I haven't seen you since that day in Manchester. You don't happen to have a cheesecake on you? Do you? I would give a barrel of oil for just one cheesecake.'

I saw we had him over a barrel. I happened to have a spare cheesecake. I always wore it round my neck on a chain as a good luck charm.

'Make it two barrels,' I said, 'and you've got yourself a deal.'

We loaded the oil on the back of our Land Rover and prepared to leave. I raised my fez, very politely.

'I say, Tommy,' sang Sir Ali, 'where did you get that hat? Where did you get that tile?'

'I got it from a TV series,' I said, 'it was called *A Fez of the Heart.'*

'Oh, my hat!' he said, and fell about.

'Why don't you stay with me,' he said, 'I can give you a job in my harem.' I wasn't up to it though.

We drove across the sand into the desert and soon ran into a queue of three-lane traffic about seven miles long. There were Rolls, Cadillacs and Buicks parked by the thousand. We found out they were waiting to use the road. Work on building it had only started the day before.

'Where is the road going?' I asked the driver of a Rolls.

'Nobody knows,' he said, 'but most of us have been waiting a year for a chance to get up into second gear. Since I bought this car last year I've got ten thousand miles on the clock. That's just backing in and out of my garage.'

When we got back to England, Mad Mick wheeled two cases of Scotch through the Customs on a trolley. It was

obvious he didn't care much for British Customs. He
went though the 'Nothing to declare' exit. He came back
for another case. He carried it on his head.

Outside, there was a sudden disturbance. It was the
Mad Brain of Britain, Brian Brain of Braintree. He was
wearing a surgical belt round his head. It was a brains-
truss. He wanted to know if anybody had any questions.
I said there was an old question to which I had never had
a satisfactory answer.

'The question is,' I asked, 'why is a mouse if it spins?'

'Ah,' said the Mad Brain of Britain, 'I see what you
mean. The usual answer is, because the higher it flies the
fewer. But I will give you the right answer.

'Suppose you're a trawler man. Would you say all the
fish you catch are net profit? It never bothers me. There
are plenty more fish in the sea. Now take my uncle, the
Mad Hatter of Hatton Garden. He always wears a Hatton
coat. He smothered his wife with diamonds. If I wanted
to smother my wife, I would use something less
expensive. Now, would you call people who serve you
cigarettes and drinks on an air liner, shop stewards? It's
all a matter of opinion. How do you know if a goldfish
likes its ant eggs hard or soft boiled? Can you tell if a
woman is a cow by her calves? If you saw a man from
Warsaw climb a flagstaff could you be sure he was a pole
squatter? Now take you. Are you aware your coat is
torn?'

'I know,' I said. 'It's a rented suit.'

'Have it your way,' he said, 'but to answer your
question about the cat.'

'The mouse,' I said.

'Yes,' said the Mad Brain of Britain, 'like I was saying,
a cross-eyed man has to watch his boots. On our coral
wedding I took my wife into a betting shop and backed a
horse in the matrimonial stakes. I won a quid. I went to
our insurance agent to take out a policy. He said "not on

115

your life". On my life, Mr Cooper, that's what he said.'

'The mouse?' I asked.

'The mouse,' he said. 'Ah yes! A lawyer met another lawyer and asked him "How's business?" The other lawyer said, "Sue, Sue." When I went to Canada I saw a huge ad on a hoarding. It said DRINK CANADA DRY. Believe me, I tried. Once in a Chinese restaurant I asked for chow-chow for desert. They brought me a dog. A friend of mine just stopped himself from falling over the edge of a volcano. Crater love hath no man. I was shipwrecked once. Lucky for me I had a bar of soap with me. I washed myself ashore. I used to have a friend. He was a dentist. His wife was a manicurist. They fought tooth and nail. When they got married I said to the bride's father, "Your son-in-law is walking like he's got lead in his pants." He said: "You're not joking. They weren't blanks I had in my shotgun.".'

'The mouse?' I asked.

'Yes,' said the Mad Brain of Britain, 'it is very discouraging.'

I know exactly how it is,' I said. 'I once saw written on a wall, "Go Home Tommy Cooper." It was on a wall of my bedroom.'

'There you are,' said the Mad Brain. 'When I was young I worked making antiques. I used to put chips on the Chippendale chairs and repair vintage mangles. Did you know that bookies always bow to their betters? That's a fact. A Sultan walked into his harem and caught a eunuch with his favourite wife. "Hands off!" he shouted and a soldier cut the eunuch's hands off. He was more cut up than ever. The point I'm trying to make is this. I'm not called the Mad Brain of Britain just for fun. Would you say you preferred a short wife to a gay one?

'If you bought a pair of houndstooth trousers, would you buy a pair with real teeth or false teeth? Now, there's a situation you won't find in the "Situations Vacant" column.'

116

'How right you are,' I said, 'but can you believe the evidence of your eyes? When I was at school I told the teacher I had seen a cow chewing the crud. She said: "You mean it was chewing the cud." I didn't bother to argue, I know what I saw. Like I saw a car in Kilburn pulling a cow. It was a cow towing.'

'I saw a cow,' said the Mad Brain, 'it was wearing a shroud. It was a cow-slip.'

'The mouse?' I said.

'I was coming to that,' said the Mad Brain of Britain. 'D'you know that in order to win my title I had to learn by heart every encyclopaedia and reference book in the British Museum. When I was a kid I was a proper quiz-kid.

'I was brained at Braintree by some of the world's best brainers, including Albert Einstein, no less. I've been in more quizzes than you've had hot dinners. I'm the most quizzical bloke in the world. I've been quizzed by the world's top quizzers and trick cyclists all the way from here to China and back again. Quizmasters? I spit 'em.

'I've been quizzed standing up and lying down and swinging from the chandelier. I've been quizzed in every language including French, Dutch and Mitch, which is a very rare language indeed. In fact it is spoken by two people, only, in the whole world. I'm one of them. The other, of course, is Mad Mitch from Mitcham. Y'know Mitch? He's the one who wrote, "Mitchmaker, Mitchmaker"; he also reports on the "Mitch of the day".

'I was a witness at a trial once at the Old Bill Bailey. Did I go before a judge? No, Tommy. Me, I had to go before a panel of judges. They asked me things like, "What is a Toxophilite and how many numismatic toxes has it got?" and personal questions like do I know my elbow from my "how's your father?"

'They asked what I knew about the Romanovs. I mentioned the great Ov family of Russian writers.

Lomonsov, Krylov, Lermantov and Nekrasov. Saltikov, Aksakov, Goncharov, and Chekhov. I, of course, added Caesar, who was the greatest Romanov of them all.

'I'm no slouch myself,' I said. 'In my business it's the quickness of the hand that deceives the eye, but my brain is pretty quick on the uptake. Like, I met a man once and right away I knew he was from the South Coast. He had a Beachy Head. I saw his friend was a South African. He was wearing a Cape of Good Hope.

'I know a man,' I continued, 'who owns wine vaults in Budapest. Yet he's not a bad chap with all his vaults. He calls his company the "Blue Danube Vaults". As a matter of fact I wanted to phone him the other day. I didn't have his number. I went to the lounge to get the A to D telephone directory. Pages B to D were missing. That's typical of the service nowadays. I dialled Diners Club instead and got the Supper Club. I gave up. But, Brain, the mouse.'

'Ah, the mouse, Tommy!' said the Mad Brain. 'Now, my dad has a small print works. He prints the small print on contracts. One day he hired an efficiency expert to come and calculate the waste level in the works. He told dad to measure all the employees, men and women, from the ground to their elbows in their stockinged feet. "I see," said dad, "thus will we arrive at the waist level. But what if the men object to wearing stockings?" "Well," said the expert, "let them wear tights".'

'Interesting,' I said, 'now hang about and I'll give you a recipe for Caribbean Banana Cake.'

'You can take it right back,' said the Mad Brain of Britain. He handed me an old chestnut.

'I don't care a bean for Caribbeans, only human beans,' he said. He gave a mad wriggle and went off singing a madrigal.

I stood for a minute wondering what that was all about. The Mad Brain always left me like that.

But it wasn't my day. There was a sudden disturbance. I heard a shot. It was the Mad Shooter from Shooters Hill. He was holding a smoking pistol and shouting, 'You'll never see Hornsey rise again.'

A man muttered something at my elbow. My elbow muttered something back. I turned round. There was a man with a black eye.

'Hello,' I said. 'What happened to you?'

'I was in this demo, wasn't I?' he said, 'and I was arrested, wasn't I? I went before the beak, didn't I? and he threw the book at me, didn't he? I've only been out a week.'

'I'm sorry,' I said.

'So you should be,' said the man. 'I mean to say, I'm a man of standing. I mean I'm a quaker.'

'Good for you,' I said. 'Let's see you quake.'

'My friends,' he said, 'I've just come from the Great National Bean Eating Contest at the Stock Exchange. I was giving a blow by blow commentary on the radio when I thought I saw this unit truss on the floor. It was just the Stockbrokers' belt.'

The quaker looked sadly after the Mad Shooter as he shot up a side street.

'And talking of mad,' said the quaker, 'in the middle of my broadcast was a sudden disturbance. It was Guy Vaux, the Mad Plotter from Vauxhall. He threw a firework at me. It was a Jumping Jack in the Baux.'

The quaker leaned over and whispered in my ear, 'I've got a chicken going cheap.'

'What do you expect it to do?' I asked. 'Bark? Anyhow, I've got a pigeon that talks.'

'Pigeons don't talk, ever,' said the quaker.

'This one does,' I said. 'It speaks pigeon English.'

'I crossed a pigeon with a toad,' said the quaker.

'I know,' I said. 'That's how you got pigeon-toed.'

'Now about this chicken,' said the quaker, pulling a

119

sorry-looking piece of poultry from under his coat.

'Careful,' I said, 'It's fowling the pavement.'

'Ah, well,' said the quaker, 'I suppose I'll have to take it with me.'

'Well, it's been nice talking to you,' I added.

He was shaking all over.

'Is anything wrong?' I asked.

'Not at all,' he said. 'Actually, I'm an earthquake.' He split with laughter and went off, his stomach rumbling.

That reminds me. It was time for dinner. I went off home. At meals, my wife always sits on my right hand. I have to eat with my left. She served soup.

'There's a funny film on this soup, dear,' I said.

'I'm sorry,' she said. 'Next time, I'll make it a western.'

I could see she was spoiling for a fight. Something had upset her.

'Well, what is it?' I asked.

'Our jade wedding,' she said. 'You didn't get me something in jade for our jade wedding.'

'Yes, I did,' I said. 'I didn't forget.'

I gave her a bottle of orangeade and ducked out fast, but not fast enough. It hit me between the shoulder blades. I felt jaded.

Well, that's my lot for now. If you want more, write to my publisher. I forget his address, but you'll find it in the book.

One thing before I go, however. Seriously, I would like to say this . . .

?

. . . uh, what's happened? Where have the lights gone? It's dark. Is this a temporary fault? I'm not finished. I haven't finished my 'seriously, I would like to say this . . .'

They've all gone home! The typesetter and the printer and the others, they're not here! I'm alone . . . I'm locked in! I can't get out. I'm stuck! I'll have to spend the night here . . . where was the coffee machine? I'll never find it in the dark . . . And I'm hungry. Famished. What's there to eat here? These typesetters live on nothing but printer's pie and alphabet soup. Very upper case. Too much mould about for my liking though.

Still, I've finished the book. Well, nearly. Now I'll be able to go on relief. They didn't give me any money last year though. I arrived there with my Stanley Gibbons album and they told me I didn't have enough stamps.

'What do you mean – six months?' I demanded. 'I've been collecting these for ten years!'

It didn't cut any ice with them. I went back the next day with a letter from my wife saying I've been collecting stamps for as long as she has known me. That didn't cut any ice either. The only thing it did cut was my standard of living.

This time I'll ask them if they have any vacancies for a writer. They're bound to have something. Writing is what I'm going to do. I'll write another book right away. I'll get someone to buy me a good pen. A special pen like Shakespeare's pen. He didn't use an ordinary pen. He used a play pen. And if it was good enough for him it will be good enough for me. I'll pen myself into a corner and come out writing. I'll re-write *Hamlet* using a biro. They'll say *that* is original, if nothing else.

Yes, that'll be the life. I'll right wrongs and right turns and disappear up a one-way street. I'll write letters to my MP and to the local paper. People will come up to me in the street and ask me for a few words. Here you are, I'll say, a few words . . . I'll take the words at random from a dictionary. This will be cheaper than Christmas presents, that's for sure.

Me becoming a writer, that will surprise quite a few people. Like my mother. She wanted me to be a dentist. I went to dentist school. The classes were held in an old converted pill box that was used by

the Home Guard in the last war.

When I left I got a job at the local surgery. I don't know why it was called the *local* surgery — I had to travel fifty miles to it every day. Still, they called the anaesthetic 'local', and that was made in Hong Kong.

The training there didn't last long. The dentist would say 'inhale', and I'd put the mask against my face and fall asleep on the floor. I couldn't stand the pain of someone having their teeth out. The thought of it makes me go steradent. Things got worse with the dentist after this. He was always threatening to fill me in. He was a big, bracing man with a mouth like Fort Knox.

I wasn't there long enough to get my dentures. I left. I was fed up to the teeth with it. But what capped it all was the day I trod on the dentist's toothpick. He crowned me. I went running home, crying all the way. I told my mother and all she said was, 'Open your mouth and let me see. Did he do it on the National Health?' No sympathy. When I told her I had left she said I would never be a Hollywood actor now. Hollywood actor? I said. Yes, like Helmet Dentine.

My aunt thought I was a failure too. She was always telling me to look at the others. I did. Young Norman, for instance. At school they said he would forge ahead. He did. He's a forger. Or Uncle Arthur — the fretworker. Working makes him fret. That's the pattern of his life. He's got a jig too. A jig saw. His life was always a puzzle to me. None of it fitted together. There was always a piece missing.

I suppose I *was* a failure to begin with.

I once became a refuse collector. I sold encyclopaedias and got refusals from everyone. I would knock on a door with twenty-four volumes under my arm and introduce myself.

'You and your encyclopaedias,' they would say, 'you think you know it all.'

Know? I didn't know what to say. So I always looked it up. It never helped. Once someone did want to buy a set. They asked me how much it would cost them. Half a minute, I said. I looked the price up in the index and couldn't find it. Three weeks later, still without having found it, they told me to move out. You call that a book of knowledge? I had no confidence it in.

Then I worked as a boxer. I started in a tea factory in Sydenham and worked my way up to fixtures at the Wembley Pool. I didn't like it there. The ice made me shiver. I gave it all up in the end – the referee was always treading on my toes. Or was it my fingers?

I was good at school though. Very good. I won the walking race three years running. Everybody was given a head start. Me? They said with feet the size of mine they would have to give me a footicap. Hands didn't enter into it.

My problem was that I never knew what I wanted to do.

I didn't get on with the teachers there. One day the teacher yelled out to me, 'Cooper, pay a little attention!' I said I was already paying as little attention as I could. He gave me fifty lines. They were all about three feet long. They were used on telegraph poles. We were studying electricity at the time and I was supposed to make something with them. The teacher gave me a lot of static too. I had to take it. I had a cold and my resistance was low. I settled for generating. I generated interest in naughty capers. The next day I was told to pay attention or else. I elsed, but the charm soon wore off. This elsing isn't all it's made out to be.

Then I answered a small ad in a paper for light house work. I got a job in a lighthouse. I was beaming, but I never could throw any light on the subject. The attraction began to dim for me after six months — there was nowhere to go at the weekends. And you were always bumping into the same people. Wherever I went the faces looked familiar. It all got a bit personal in the end. The other keepers there were coming up to me and telling me to trim my wick. I ask you. I'd had enough of it.

The beach there wasn't very good either. There was sand all right but the tide was always in. When my bucket and spade were swept out to sea I could never find anywhere to buy a new set.

The amusement arcades were not much to write home about either. In fact there was only one slot machine. And that was always engaged. It was hardly enough to keep the mind alive.

On Saturday nights we used to hold dances. We'd festoon the main hall with decorations, move the chairs back, make sandwiches, open a few bottles of sea-water. But no one ever turned up. We would end the evening sitting around filling in forms for computer dating clubs. Sometimes we would fill in the forms for each other.

This way we'd all get the chance of meeting the type of ladies we wouldn't normally meet. It never worked though. By the time the bottles arrived back to tell us where to meet them it was too late.

I decided that it was time I moved on. I packed my bags, went out to the rocks and began hitching for a lift. I'd made myself a little sign with the word MAINLAND painted on it. A ship finally stopped. It was going to Scotland. It was a tramp steamer. I knew it was a tramp steamer the moment I climbed aboard. The captain was a tramp. The engineer was a

tramp. The first mate was a tramp. And I never got to meet the barmaid, she always had her hands full.

My nautical experience would come in handy at last. I'd once been a shipwrong. That's what they call a shipwright who never does anything properly. It wasn't easy. I had a very important job in the yards. I used to wash and iron the ribbon that the champagne bottle was swung on. I was fired for damaging company property. The foreman told me to punch the clock in the mornings. Well, they did cover it in glass. What do you expect?

I had a good time sailing back. One of the deck hands was Australian. He once crossed a kangaroo with sheep. He got a woolly jumper.

There was an Arab on board too. He was big in oil. He was even bigger when he got out of it. He let me into the great Arabian money secret – they keep it all in sandbanks. It sounded a bit shifty to me. You would never know where it was. He told me that in the desert your money, unlike time, never runs out. I wasn't arguing. He had a duneful. He used an egg-timer for a purse.

The navigator was a strange man. He was always plotting. He was in cohorts with the cook, another strange man. I once saw the cook on the main deck shouting at a bunch of carrots. He was taking them on a root march.

The engineer was rum too. Though he swore blind he was a teetotaler. He carried a cane and always stirred his tea with it. It was a sugar cane. The stokers thought he was sweet. He once asked me if I had a sweet tooth. No, I said. But I rummaged through my pockets and offered him a bull's eye instead. He didn't talk to me after that.

After a week we docked at Aberdeen. I climbed ashore and soon found my hand-legs. They were in

my overnight bag along with my toothbrush, comb and boot polish. I knew I couldn't have left them on board.

I made straight for a restaurant. I sat around and no one took any notice of me.

'How do you get a glass of water in here?' I asked.

'Set yourself on fire,' said the man at the next table.

It was an inflammable situation and I was smouldering. A young lady asked me if I had a light. It was beginning to add up. I produced a lighter from behind her ear. She could see that I was no match for her. Her cigarette was soon enflamed. She wasn't, but her cigarette was.

The waiter finally arrived. He'd been out to lunch.

'What do you recommend?' I asked.

'The restaurant next door,' he said, appetisingly.

I needed no second telling.

Next door I bumped into a man wearing a pair of Jean's. She was wearing a pair of his. They both looked at me.

'Let's go riding,' she said hoarsely.

'I'm falling for you,' he stumbled.

'I'm only here for the kidneys and chips,' I added liverishly.

They rushed out of the place.

I sat down and had a slap-up meal. It wasn't cooked very well. But the slapping-up was done to perfection.

I got talking to two crooks. They had just been involved in a bank robbery that had gone wrong. They were all set to blow the safe when one of them ran out of puff.

'Have you got the jelly?' one said.

'No,' the other replied, 'I couldn't get any but I've brought some custard instead.'

They were true professionals. Then they decided to crack the safe, but no one had a spoon with them so they gave it up.

They both eyed me.

'Cooper,' they said, 'are you a fence?'

I was puzzled at first, but then I realised it was a compliment. After all these years it makes a change from people thinking you look like a brick outhouse.

Then they asked me the question again. I didn't know what to say. I finally showed them a picture of the Great Wall of China. Would this do? They took the snap away and looked at it carefully.

'Is this heavily guarded?' they asked. 'Where is the night-watchman's hut?'

I didn't know. They left saying as soon as they could get it they would look me up.

After settling the Bill in the restaurant – I gave him some indigestion tablets – I struck out for the Highlands. Whistling and singing:

Old King Cole was a merry old soul
And on that we all agree,
But he never did call for his pipe and his bowl,
But for a fag and a cup of tea.

A very catchy tune. I caught it off my uncle, along with a cold. In fact I still get a cold whenever I sing it. It's infectious too. I had to put it in quarantine for six months before I could use it. I wouldn't mind, but it is not even funny.

On the way out I passed a stadium. It was a dog track. I'd never been in one before. My family were always telling me I was going to the dogs. Now I had arrived.

In the first race I backed the dog in trap five. It was some trap. He didn't get out of it. Well, it wouldn't

have mattered if he had. The race was won by a rabbit. It was one of those very fast Scottish rabbits. A jock rabbit. Somebody said it was won by a hare. It wasn't true. The rabbit was about thirty yards ahead of the first dog. Anyone could see that.

When the bookies wouldn't take a bet on the rabbits I decided it was time I continued on my way. I was soon in the Highlands and looking for a job. I became a forester. It was my big opportunity to tell the wood from the trees. I was employed as a shouter. I had to shout 'Timber!' after the trees had hit the ground.

I never worked quite so hard in all my life. That first night I slept like a log. I know I slept like a log because when I woke up in the morning I was in the fireplace.

The other foresters were an unfriendly lot. They didn't take to me. They were always telling me that I was going against the grain. I told them to get knotted. They didn't like that. After six months of this I began to pine for the old life – so I soon saw through this job and moved on.

I then found a job on a big estate in the mountains. I was the gamekeeper. I was in charge of the ludo, the snakes-and-ladders, the tiddly-winks and the Monopoly. I lived in the cupboard under the stairs. I soon handed my notice in. The people above me made so much noise I never could get to sleep at nights.

It was time I got married and left this roving life. I married my wife because I thought she was worth her weight in gold. If she is, she has never paid out. She told me our licence gave her the right to drive me. She has, to the ends of the earth. She married me for much the same reason, money. But then she found out that I had spent it all on her before we got married. She wasn't pleased.

But I have enjoyed my life. I've done what I've wanted. And now I can become a writer. My wife thinks I'll make a lovely writer. I thinks she's lovely too. She also thinks I remind her of her father. I don't. He liked German wine a lot. I don't. He was always disappearing down to the hock shop.

My wife once bought a pot of face cream. It was guaranteed to remove the wrinkles from a prune. It did nothing for her but we've always had the smoothest prunes ever with our custard.

Oooh! I feel so strong I could crush a grape. I feel sleepy too. Spending the night in a print works! What time do they open up? I'm going to nod off, I am. I'd better just finish this. The publishers said it was going to be a limited edition. Limited to as many copies as they can sell. They got the idea from my manuscript. They said it was the limit. But back to the work in hand. I've got to put in something serious at the end of this book. Something serious like . . . like . . . uh . . . Yes, something serious.

Uh-huh. Here goes —

'Seriously, I would like to say . . .'

What's this? The pen's running out of ink. Oh, no!

'Seriously, I would like . . . .

Appendix One

MY PUBLISHER phoned me late last night to say he had a little space left over. He asked me if I would like to write a few more words. Yes, I replied, but don't ask me what they mean.

Abaddon, fiked, filaceous, hendiadys, nid-nod, mangonel, norroy, lannaret, quirt, quinte, primp, squaloid, lyke, machan, noumenon, fal-al, gabelle, moidore, planxty, nutate, hiccatee, pirogue, horresco referens, vinasse, vigoroso.

Stephanite, stegnosis, stearin, sponsal, spole, spleuchan, polyrhizous, myrobalan, jaconet, hyaloid, gestalt, pachisi, sasin, sarothrum, transire, undose, rhysimeter, rhyolite, polverine, patella, patibulary, orchesis, mutograph, monad, macarize, hierurgy, hidrotic, epitasis.

Epitonic, galiongee, galimatias, monobasic, oxytone, percoct, pillau, sealyham, succades, yorkshire pudding, subsultus, precentor, peccary, hidalgo, heulandite.

Abaddon, fiked, filaceous, hendiadys, nid-nod, mangonel, norroy, lannaret, quirt . . ..

I gave up just before sunrise. I was beginning to feel I was repeating myself. It was no use. This would have to do. Anyway, I have to wake my wife up at the crack of dawn with a cup of tea. I throw it over her and say, 'Where's my breakfast?' Actually, I don't really. *She* throws it over me . . .

Appendix Two

A FEW YEARS AGO, give or take a memory lapse, I was interviewed on television. I like talking, and talk I did. I didn't say much but I more than made up for it with the talking. I'm a master of the meaningful silence. A wizard at the meaningless utterance. I always break the ice at parties with my stimulating conversation, and when I've done that I break the glasses too. I don't mean to but it just happens. Everybody has always asked me for a few words. My parents were always asking me for 'please' and 'thank you'. My wife never tires of hearing me say, 'Yes, dear. You *do* need it.' It has never been any different.

GET BACK ONTO THE SUBJECT – *Editor*

Sorry, I wandered. Where am I? I've never been here before in my life. Where is this?

YOU'RE IN THE APPENDIX

But I had that out years ago.

THIS IS THE BOOK'S APPENDIX

I can hear a strange musical sound in this book. It's been worrying me.

WHAT SOUND IS IT?

Footnotes!

ENOUGH! THERE NOW FOLLOWS A TRANSCRIPT OF A TELEVISION INTERVIEW WITH TOMMY COOPER RECORDED IN THE 1960s . . .

INTERVIEWER: Mr Cooper, I would first of all like to thank

you for joining us this evening.

TOMMY: Thank you. Thank you very much. Thank you.

INTERVIEWER: Now, I would like to talk to you today about your artistic influences. When did you first realise you were of an artistic temperament?

TOMMY: My mother. I was only five at the time. She was a teetotaler. She used to take me to meetings of the local temperance group. They all said I was very artful.

INTERVIEWER: Why was that?

TOMMY: Because I used to slip out of the hall before the meeting got going.

INTERVIEWER: I see.

TOMMY: My teacher said I was artful too. Everyone said I was artful. When I left home, at my first digs, they called me the 'artful lodger'. It was a very artistic household but I was always very lonely there. I was always asking for Maur.

INTERVIEWER: Moore? Henry Moore, the sculptor?

TOMMY: No. *Maur.* Maureen Green. She was the landlady's daughter. I never actually met her. I only ever heard about her.

INTERVIEWER: Yes.

TOMMY: She had a grate reputation. In front of the fireplace, anywhere, they were always talking about her. The other lodgers tried to tell me she was a cleaning lady

152

or something, that she worked in a laundry. I knew she was a nurse though.

INTERVIEWER: What became of her?

TOMMY: She became a singer much later. She made some records and had a couple of big hits on her hands.

INTERVIEWER: Now perhaps we could move onto books?

TOMMY: Huh . . . I'm quite happy in this chair, honestly.

INTERVIEWER: Mr Cooper, you've always been quite fond of books.

TOMMY: Fond? Yes, very fond. I was always fondling something or other. I was much younger then, I was.

INTERVIEWER: Can you think of any books that made a notable impression on you?

TOMMY: There was one.

INTERVIEWER: Which was?

TOMMY: No, I tell a lie. There were two . . .

INTERVIEWER: Two books made a notable impression on you?

TOMMY: Yes, two. Can I go now?

INTERVIEWER: Mr Cooper, the interview has hardly begun . . .

TOMMY: Oh! No one explained.

INTERVIEWER: Now what were these two books?

TOMMY: Which two?

INTERVIEWER: The two that made a notable impression on you, Mr Cooper.

TOMMY: Those two!

INTERVIEWER: Yes. Those two.

TOMMY: I can't remember.

INTERVIEWER: Well, they hardly made a big impression on you then, did they?

TOMMY: No, they *did* make a big impression on me.

INTERVIEWER: Mr Cooper, you are a sane, intelligent human being.

TOMMY: I'm sorry. I forgot.

INTERVIEWER: What were these two books?

TOMMY: How long do I get?

INTERVIEWER: What?

TOMMY: How long do I get to answer the question?

INTERVIEWER: This is not a quiz programme.

TOMMY: No, I didn't mean that. I don't know why I said it. I shouldn't have asked the question.

INTERVIEWER: Good. We're getting somewhere at last.

TOMMY: What I meant to say was . . . uh . . . You say this isn't a quiz programme?

INTERVIEWER: Yes. I said this isn't a quiz programme.

TOMMY: Good. I don't like quiz programmes.

INTERVIEWER: What were the two programmes?

TOMMY: *Programmes?*

INTERVIEWER: I mean books.

TOMMY: You're talking about books again.

INTERVIEWER: I know I'm talking about books again! Just what were the two books that made such an impression on you?

TOMMY: I don't know. I give up. What's the answer?

INTERVIEWER: Mr Cooper, you are doing your best to provoke me.

TOMMY: Scout's honour I'm not! Honestly.

INTERVIEWER: I'm not going to lose my temper.

TOMMY: Good. I like a man who knows his own mind.

INTERVIEWER: Let me start again.

TOMMY: Yes, it is rather hot today, isn't it?

INTERVIEWER: And I would like simple and direct answers to these questions, Mr Cooper.

TOMMY: No trick questions?

INTERVIEWER: You like reading?

TOMMY: I like reading.

INTERVIEWER: Good. First base.

TOMMY: What sort of question is that?

INTERVIEWER: What books made a notable impression on you?

TOMMY: Take a card. Any card. Don't look at it. Don't show it to me. Just put it in your pocket.

INTERVIEWER: *&!!%**&*

TOMMY: No, don't be silly. Come on. Take a card.

INTERVIEWER: I don't know why I'm interviewing you.

TOMMY: Just take a card. Yes, that's right. Now put it straight into your pocket.

INTERVIEWER: Okay!

TOMMY: Good. Now what two books made a notable impression on me?

INTERVIEWER: Uh . . . yes.

TOMMY: I'll tell you. They were *The Decline of the West*

by Oswald Spengler and Morley's biography of Lord Gladstone.

INTERVIEWER: *Very* interesting. Neither is the sort of book that one would . . . uh . . . *immediately* associate with you, Mr Cooper.

TOMMY: That's as maybe.

INTERVIEWER: That's as maybe.

TOMMY: But whenever I misbehaved in the history lesson the school teacher would tell me to bend over and whack me with whatever was nearest. They made a big impression on me. A *very* big impression.

INTERVIEWER: Mr Cooper, are you trying to make an ass out of me?

TOMMY: Abracadabra – Abracadee. *Zooph!*

INTERVIEWER: *Most* amusing.

TOMMY: Oh! You're still you I see.

INTERVIEWER: Very much so.

TOMMY: That trick cost me 25p. I bought it a year ago. This was the first time I've used it. The guarantee only lasted six months.

INTERVIEWER: I'm only going to ask you one more question, *Mr* Cooper.

TOMMY: Friday's out. I always wash my hair that night.

INTERVIEWER: Could we be serious just for one moment?

TOMMY: That's a poor question. I thought you would at least ask me something about Greek philosophy.

INTERVIEWER: If I thought for a second that you knew anything about Greek philosophy we would discuss it.

TOMMY: I know plenty . . .

INTERVIEWER: For example?

TOMMY: You name something and I'll tell you what he says about it.

INTERVIEWER: He? There was more than one Greek philosopher, I seem to recall.

TOMMY: Was there? I know only the one.

INTERVIEWER: Plato? Socrates? Heraclitus?

TOMMY: No. Aristotle.

INTERVIEWER: Ah! Aristotle.

TOMMY: We call him Ari for short.

INTERVIEWER: *Very* familiar.

TOMMY: He wouldn't have us call him anything else.

INTERVIEWER: Aristotle has been dead for two thousand years!

TOMMY: He has been looking a little under the weather lately.

INTERVIEWER: Who are you talking about? Tell me *that!*

TOMMY: Ari Galapagos.

INTERVIEWER: Ari *Galapagos!?*

TOMMY: Yes. He has the best kebab stall in Victoria. The kebabs are out of this world. He never has any in stock. The moussaka sundae is a sight for sore eyes. Don't try eating it, but if you have tired or sore eyes it'll work wonders. His speciality though is the cheese and tomato sandwich . . . if the bread's available, that is. If it isn't, well, he'll give you a tomato and a postcard of the Cheddar Gorge. You can gorge yourself on *that*. Very filling.

INTERVIEWER: And what pearls of wisdom can Mr Ari Galapagos offer?

TOMMY: All sorts of things. He has views on everything. He's very good on business philosophy.

INTERVIEWER: Yes?

TOMMY: Old Greek proverbs like 'When the winds echo in the cash register the olive tree withers'.

INTERVIEWER: I really think I've heard enough.

TOMMY: 'The salad dressing which shuns the oil has no oil.'

INTERVIEWER: Was that directed at me?

TOMMY: 'Ask not for whom the moussaka overcooks. It overcooks for thee.'

INTERVIEWER: I should have learnt my lesson by now, *Mr* Cooper.

TOMMY: 'Once kebabed. Twice frittered.'

INTERVIEWER: Enough of this. You've demonstrated to our viewers this evening – quite conclusively, I may add – that your intelligence is on a par with your conjuring ability.

TOMMY: I knew I'd forgotten something.

INTERVIEWER: Now in case there are any lingering doubts in the minds of our audience I propose to ask you one final question.

TOMMY: I told you, I wash my hair on Friday nights.

INTERVIEWER: Who, Mr Cooper, is the present Queen of England?

TOMMY: That's a tough question.

INTERVIEWER: To you it may be.

TOMMY: Can I confer on this one?

INTERVIEWER: You can do whatever you like as long as you give me an answer in one minute.

TOMMY: No one told me I was going to be asked a question like that.

INTERVIEWER: You have forty-five seconds left.

TOMMY: Take that card out of your pocket.

160

INTERVIEWER: Very well. Forty seconds . . .

TOMMY: What card is it?

INTERVIEWER: The Queen of Hearts. Thirty seconds . . .

TOMMY: Now turn the card over.

INTERVIEWER: Twenty seconds . . .

TOMMY: What is written in the corner?

INTERVIEWER: Uh . . . ten sec-!

TOMMY: Yes!

INTERVIEWER: The name ELIZABETH!

TOMMY: There you are. Queen Elizabeth.

INTERVIEWER: But it's a trick.

TOMMY: That's the name of the game!

INTERVIEWER: But . . .

TOMMY: Fancy a cheese and tomato at Ari Galapagos' stall?

INTERVIEWER: What a good idea.

TOMMY: Yes, come on. We'll drink a drink as well.

Bibliography

M Y PUBLISHER SAID a bibliography gives a book a bit of respectability. I was in no position to argue (I was doing handstands at the time).

What follows is more a list of suggested further reading. It includes some lovely books by and about my ancestors, books from my childhood, a few items I picked up in a jumble sale the week before last and a couple of overdue volumes from the local library.

BROWN, ELPHINSTONE. *Tiny Tales for Tiny People.* Godalming, 1932.
Adventure Stories for Boys. Portsmouth, 1933.
Tales of Action for Young Men. Aldershot, 1934.
Your Twenty-first Birthday Book of Thrills and Spills. Leeds, 1935.
Tough Tales for the Tough. Liverpool, 1936.
Spicy Tales for the Adult. Soho, 1937.
I collected all these books. My mother never let me get the ones published in 1938 and 1939 though.

COOPER, AUGUSTUS. *Tips on the Manly Art of Manfolding.* Benares, 1870.
This was written by my great-grandfather. He was in the Indian Army. He was a great scout and explorer. He disappeared in 1872, in Beccles, after going to get a paper. He supposedly reappeared in Doncaster in 1880 clutching a battered copy of *The Times* and enquiring,

A simple gadget my grandfather invented for the vanishing card trick.

'Is this the Beccles road?'

COOPER, ERNEST. *How to Build your own Flying Bomb*. Grimsby, 1942
How to Convert your Anderson Shelter into a Nuclear Reactor. New Mexico, 1944.
The Fire-watcher's Origami Manual. Boreham Wood, 1945.
Crocheting your Way to Victory. Preston, 1945.
Private Munitions Manufacture for Fun and Profit. Tufnell Park, 1945.
A 1001 Things to Make and Do with String now that the War has Ended. Potsdam, 1946.
Ernest, a distant cousin many times removed (principally to places of detention), was the most prolific of the writing Coopers. He authored many other pamphlets including the justly acclaimed, *Can your Cat Foretell your Future Love and Happiness in the Stars?* He retired to his seaside cottage in Rutland last year and now devotes his spare time to atomic fission.

COOPER, PHILOMENON. *True Arts of Magycke Extoll'd*. Margate, 1666.
Phil wrote the first book in the English language on conjuring. He also ghosted stage plays for a theatrical fop called Will Shaxpur.

COOPER, VICTORIA. *What Every Young Magician Should Know About Etiquette*. Cheltenham, 1888.
For many years this was the only volume explaining the social graces to the conjuring profession. Throughout the last twenty years of the nineteenth century magicians couldn't do any tricks but they were the best behaved stage performers ever.

SIWECKI, JULIAN. *London Worthies: From Canute to Cooper.* London, 1974.

Modesty forbids me mentioning anything more about this very great work on those illustrious and accomplished residents of this famed city.

STENCIL, HERBERT. *The Coopers of Ongar: Records of a Yeoman Family.* Venice, 1923.

Who they were and where they came from. The rise of one of the most notable English families. Written by the author of *How to Climb Your Family Tree*.

YEBBLE, PERCY. *The Senior Citizens' Book of Cacti.* York, 1973.

Written by a man who once bought me a drink in Bristol in 1951.

URBAN MYTHS
Phil Healey and Rick Glanvill

This hilarious collection of contemporary 'true stories' unleashes over 200 new, borrowed and blue urban myths, starring the ubiquitous 'friend-of-a-friend'. They're saucy, implausible, bizarre and sometimes scary – and as with all the best yarns, they have a spooky ring of truth. In a society obsessed by gossip, *Urban Myths* are the best unfounded stories around. Read them here and never trust that 'No, but it really happened' line again.

ISBN 0 86369 686 4

THE RETURN OF URBAN MYTHS
Phil Healey and Rick Glanvill

More incredible but 'true' stories of sex, drink and unreliable machinery – featuring the live Xmas turkey, the Mexican tobacco pouch, and over 200 other astounding 'friend-of-a-friend' classics. A glowing testament to the sordid inventiveness of the human mind, this new literary twist on an age-old form plumbs the depths of society's irrational prejudices, unquenchable gullibility and sheer stupidity. Spice up any conversation with this fresh and fruity cocktail of comical cautionary tales.

ISBN 0 86369 752 6

URBAN MYTHS – UNPLUGGED
Phil Healey and Rick Glanvill

They said it could never be done, but here it is . . . the third, acoustic version of the best-selling *Urban Myths* series. You split your sides with the first, bust a blood vessel over the second, so go ahead, snap a gusset with *Unplugged*. Once again, Messrs Healey and Glanvill pay tribute to the fiendish storytelling genius of humankind, gathering together mad, bad and dangerous examples of downright daftness. All human life is here, and quite a few animals too.

ISBN 0 86369 897 2